HEAVEN AND NEW JERUSALEM

A Biblically-Accurate Survey of the City of God
and Life in the Kingdom

JARÓD MURPHEY

GLASS MOUNTAINS
PUBLISHERS

Heaven and New Jerusalem:
A Biblically Accurate Survey of the City of God and Life in the Kingdom
© 2025 by Jaród Murphey

All rights reserved. No portion of this book may be reproduced, stored in a retrieval system, or transmitted in any form or by any means (electronic, mechanical, photocopy, recording, or any other) except for brief quotations in printed reviews without the prior permission of the publisher.

Glass Mountains Publishers
820 W Danforth Rd
Unit #476
Edmond, OK 73003

ISBN: 979-8-218-70906-8

Scripture quotations taken from the (NASB®) New American Standard Bible®, Copyright © 1960, 1971, 1977, 1995 by The Lockman Foundation. Used by permission. All rights reserved. lockman.org

Dedicated to my wife.

Only an amazing God could bless me with a woman like you, virtuous and beautiful in every way—your worth is far above jewels. For now, you are honored in this book about New Jerusalem, but in the future, you will be honored in the great City itself.

Acknowledgements:

I owe a lot to Janet Willis (who wrote *What on Earth is Heaven Like? The New Creation and the New Jerusalem*) and Randy Alcorn (who wrote *Heaven: A Comprehensive Guide to Everything the Bible Says About Our Eternal Home*). Willis' book helped convince me of the timing of the descent of New Jerusalem and Alcorn's book helped me fall in love with my future Heavenly home. I cannot recommend their work enough.

Table of Contents

Introduction — 1

Chapter I: The Restoration of Earth — 17

Chapter II: The Presence of the Saints on Earth During the Millennium — 31

Chapter III: The Descent of New Jerusalem at the Beginning of the Millennium — 41

Chapter IV: The Millennial Temple — 71

Chapter V: The Lives of the Saints in Heaven and New Jerusalem — 85

Chapter VI: The Geography and Society of Heaven and New Jerusalem — 121

Bibliography — 146

Heaven and New Jerusalem

INTRODUCTION

It's a heartbreaking reality: when most people imagine Heaven, they often think of disembodied, angelic, ghost-like figures, draped in white, plucking harps on clouds, stuck in an endless church service. This idea is so utterly uninspiring and boring that the prospect of enduring this reality for all eternity can actually bring people to tears. We were crafted by God, the good Creator of all things, to yearn for the thrill of adventure, the warmth of community, the richness of culture, the challenge of overcoming obstacles, the satisfaction of meaningful work, and yes, even the goodness of fun and pleasure.

When we're given the impression that Heaven will be empty of all these vibrant elements, it sparks a deep-seated fear within us about that destination, and we lose our desire for it. While some might still choose an eternity of sheer dullness in Heaven simply because the alternative is the torment of Hell, tragically far too many in our society have decided that Hell would be better. They have been led to believe that Hell, of all places, would offer a more exciting and enjoyable experience than the tedious, never-ending routine of worship and singing in Heaven.

It's truly one of Satan's most cunning and effective schemes: convincing humanity that Heaven is a place of boredom. Christians who swallow this deception end up living miserable lives now, shackled by a fear of death and robbed of any real motivation to live in light of eternity. Those who don't know Christ, who fall for this same lie, use it as a convenient excuse to reject the free and glorious gift of eternal life that God offers.

The Devil, the god of this present age (2 Corinthians 4:4), has been tirelessly working for thousands of years to craft this narrative, and sadly, he has been remarkably successful. The roots of this lie go far back, all the way to ancient gnostic heresies that slithered their way into the early church. Those gnostic snakes taught that the material world around us was inherently evil, while only the spiritual world was inherently good. Because of this warped view, they denied the beautiful truth that God would physically raise His saints from the dead and bring this material earth to a state of perfect restoration. Instead, they presented a belief that true existence was disembodied, immaterial spirituality. Ever since, the church and Christianized societies have struggled with the lingering poison of this gnostic mindset.

Elements of this kind of thinking found their way into Medieval, Renaissance, and Enlightenment era paintings, which

Heaven and New Jerusalem

often depicted Heaven as a ghostly, spiritual realm floating in the clouds. These misleading drawings, in turn, influenced the portrayal of Heaven in countless books, movies, and television shows throughout the 1900s and 2000s. These depictions are largely responsible for the deep misunderstandings that people still have about Heaven today.

What if I told you that this lie—this notion that Heaven is a boring, immaterial, spiritual, never-ending church service—couldn't be further from the truth? God's own Word speaks volumes about the rich details of daily life in the city of New Jerusalem and the coming new heaven and earth. Truly, it's anything but dull. Our primary purpose in Heaven will be to rule and reign with Christ over the nations, as kings and queens in His

global government, forever and ever (Daniel 7:27, Revelation 2:26-27, and Revelation 22:5). On top of that, we will serve God (Revelation 22:3) using the gifts and passions He designed in us.

Woven through it all, there will be immense enjoyment, fun, and pleasure. David, speaking through the Holy Spirit, wrote this about God: "In Your presence is fullness of joy; in Your right hand there are pleasures forever" (Psalm 16:11). Similarly, Paul described God as the One "who richly supplies us with all things to enjoy" (1 Timothy. 6:17). If that weren't enough, those who are in Christ will never again taste death, mourning, or pain (Revelation 21:4). Instead of fear, worry, and anxiety, we will experience a peace that passes understanding. Instead of sorrow, we will be filled with a happiness beyond our wildest dreams. Instead of boredom and loneliness, we will have adventure and deep community. Does that sound dull? Or does it sound like the best news you've ever heard?

It is vitally important, for the sake of our walk in this life, to meditate on the realities of Heaven. Philippians 4:8 urges us,

> Finally, brethren, whatever is true, whatever is honorable, whatever is right, whatever is pure, whatever is lovely, whatever is of good repute, if there is any excellence and if anything worthy of praise, dwell on these things.

Similarly, Colossians 3:1-4 exhorts,

> Therefore if you have been raised up with Christ, keep seeking the things above, where Christ is, seated at the right hand of God. Set your mind on the things above, not on the things that are on earth. For you have died and your life is hidden with Christ in God. When Christ, who is our life, is revealed, then you also will be revealed with Him in glory.

One important reason for why we should set our minds on the coming Kingdom of Heaven can be found in 2 Peter 3:11-13, which says,

> Since all these things are to be destroyed in this way, what sort of people ought you to be in holy conduct and godliness, looking for and hastening the coming of the day of God, because of which the heavens will be destroyed by burning, and the elements will melt with intense heat! But according to His promise we are looking for new heavens and a new earth, in which righteousness dwells.

This passage tells us that "looking for and hastening the coming of the day of God," a day that will result in the destruction of the ungodly and the creation of a righteous new heavens and earth, fuels our desire to live holy and godly lives. When we truly grasp the wrath that awaits those who reject God and the fleeting nature of sin's empty promises in this life, how can we possibly choose to remain in sin? When we begin to understand the pleasure, blessings, and rewards that God will lavish in Heaven—a

Heaven and New Jerusalem

place of pure happiness and adventure—on the righteous who pursue good works, how much more will this thought ignite our hearts to love and good deeds? When we contemplate Heaven, we're not just motivated to do good things in this life to gain more

rewards there, but we also overflow with love and thankfulness to God because of the glorious reality He is preparing for us. And that is a powerful motivator, indeed.

In the same way, the knowledge of Heaven and the city of New Jerusalem can act as an anchor for our souls, preventing us from clinging too tightly to the fleeting things of this present world. It can infuse us with a holy boldness, a willingness to step out in faith and pursue the things that we know God is calling us to do. Hebrews 11:8-16 beautifully illustrates this truth, saying,

> By faith Abraham, when he was called, obeyed by going out to a place which he was to receive for an inheritance; and he went out, not knowing where he was going. By faith he lived as an alien in the land of promise,

Heaven and New Jerusalem

as in a foreign land, dwelling in tents with Isaac and Jacob, fellow heirs of the same promise; *for he was looking for the city which has foundations, whose architect and builder is God.* By faith even Sarah herself received ability to conceive, even beyond the proper time of life, since she considered Him faithful who had promised. Therefore there was born even of one man, and him as good as dead at that, as many descendants as the stars of heaven in number, and innumerable as the sand which is by the seashore.

All these died in faith, without receiving the promises, but having seen them and having welcomed them from a distance, and having confessed that they were strangers and exiles on the earth. *For those who say such things make it clear that they are seeking a country of their own.* And indeed if they had been thinking of that country from which they went out, they would have had opportunity to return. *But as it is, they desire a better country, that is, a heavenly one. Therefore God is not ashamed to be called their God; for He has prepared a city for them.* (emphasis added)

This world, in its present brokenness, is not our lasting residence. We are wayfarers and pilgrims passing through. Our chief allegiance, our true citizenship, is in Heaven alone (Philippians 3:20). Therefore, our deepest longing, our heart's truest desire, should be to align ourselves with the will of the King of our celestial homeland. Think of it this way: with New Jerusalem as our ultimate destination, we are, in a very real sense, an occupying force in enemy territory, ambassadors on a vital mission for our King. C.S. Lewis, with his characteristic brilliance, captured this truth when he described our situation:

> Enemy-occupied territory—that is what this world is. Christianity is the story of how the rightful king has landed, you might say landed in disguise, and is calling us all to take part in a great campaign of sabotage.[1]

A soldier stationed behind enemy lines doesn't settle in comfortably, does he? There's a tension, an awareness of the conflict. So it is with us. This world, under the sway of the evil one, can never fully satisfy us. Our hearts yearn for the day when the enemy is vanquished, when Christ's kingdom fully triumphs, and when we can, at last, experience the fullness of joy and purpose that we were created for. And oh, how the reality of Heaven can anchor us when life crashes in! Remember Jesus' words to His disciples, spoken in anticipation of His death and resurrection in John 16:20-22:

> Truly, truly, I say to you, that you will weep and lament, but the world will rejoice; you will grieve, but your grief will be turned into joy. Whenever a woman is in labor she has pain, because her hour has come; but when she gives birth

Heaven and New Jerusalem

to the child, she no longer remembers the anguish because of the joy that a child has been born into the world. Therefore you too have grief now; but I will see you again, and your heart will rejoice, and no one will take your joy away from you.

In the midst of life's fiercest trials, when pain seems unbearable—like the disciples' despair at the cross, or the agony of childbirth—it's the hope of what awaits us that sustains us. Just as the mother finds joy in the child, knowing the pain is temporary, so we find hope in the certain future: we will see Jesus, and we will experience the unparalleled glory and wonder of Heaven. This knowledge gives us hope and strength so that we can persevere through hardship.

Heaven and New Jerusalem

In the chapters that follow, we will study many Biblically-available details of God's coming Kingdom, helping us set our minds on Heaven and the "things above." By the end of the book, you will be able to answer the following intriguing questions: what will our lives look like in Heaven? Will we have meaningful work to do in this new world? What will our relationship with our earthly spouses be like? Will we have friends and fun activities to enjoy? Will we be confined to this planet for eternity, or will we explore new worlds? What will society look like in God's new creation? What elements of geography will be the same or different in the new earth? Will aspects of our nations and cultures (e.g, music, clothing, dancing, literature, food, and architecture) be present in Heaven? In what ways will they change? What will happen to the nation and people of Israel?

I will also use scriptural evidence to build a case for the following eschatological timeline, a correct comprehension of which is crucial to understand what awaits us: following the glorious wedding feast in Heaven, Jesus will return to earth, accompanied by His vast and victorious army, a company consisting of all the saints and angels. Jesus and His heavenly host will engage the Antichrist and his armies in the battle of Armageddon, utterly eradicating all the evildoers who have followed after him.

Heaven and New Jerusalem

In the aftermath of this triumph, God will perform a magnificent work of restoration, creating a new heaven and new earth. New Jerusalem will descend, causing Heaven to fully invade earth and become joined to it, a glorious merging of the two realms. In His mercy, God will preserve the lives of many mortals: individuals who were not Christians prior to the rapture, but who survived the Day of the Lord because they refused to bow down to the Antichrist. These humans will enter the Kingdom of Heaven and will repopulate the earth, which was decimated by God's judgments (Isaiah 13:12), with mortal offspring.

However, even in this era of blessing, some of the descendants of these mortals will choose wickedness, failing to be thankful for God's abundant grace. These individuals will be judged by God and struck down at a young age, as Isaiah 65:20 foretells. This same verse also assures us that mortal infants and children will no longer die in the Kingdom. Righteous mortals, it appears, will also live until the end of the Millennium, at which time their bodies will be transformed instantaneously, in the same manner as those who were raptured a thousand years earlier.

During the Millennium, Jesus will reign as King from New Jerusalem. His immortal saints will serve as members of His government, sharing in His rule over the nations. At the end of one thousand years, Satan will be released for a brief period to deceive the wicked among the nations. These deceived multitudes will attack New Jerusalem, but God will miraculously destroy them with fire.

Following this final rebellion, all the wicked who have ever lived will be resurrected and stand before God at the Great White Throne Judgment. There, they will be judged according to their deeds and sentenced to an eternity in the Lake of Fire. At last, having conquered every enemy, Christ will deliver the Kingdom to God the Father. Death, the final enemy, will be abolished, and from that point forward, there will be no more death in all of creation, forever and ever. To celebrate this ultimate victory, a grand banquet, a feast of rejoicing, will be prepared for all peoples, as described in Isaiah 25:6-8. This is the culmination of God's plan,

the glorious finale of the drama of redemption. A timeline filled with both judgment and grace, a testament to God's unwavering love and His ultimate triumph over all evil.

And what lies beyond this? What awaits us after the culmination of the Millennium? While certain aspects of the Millennial Reign, such as God's rule from New Jerusalem, the existence of the earth, and the presence of nations, will likely endure after the Millennium, much of the age which comes after this remains shrouded in mystery. But let us not be troubled by this veil of the unknown. God has prepared us to be participants in an amazing story, a narrative that stretches eternally into the future.

It is impossible for us, with our finite minds, to grasp every detail of the infinite grand design He has woven for us. However, we can hold fast to certain truths. Most significantly, we can be confident that those of us who are saints will live eternally (John 3:16) and that love will last forever (Psalm 136 and 1 Corinthians 13:8, 13). We also know that throughout "the ages to come," God will lavish upon us the riches of His grace and kindness. Ephesians 2:4-7 assures us,

> But God, being rich in mercy, because of His great love with which He loved us, even when we were dead in our transgressions, made us alive together with Christ (by grace you have been saved), and raised us up with Him, and seated us with Him in the heavenly places in Christ Jesus,

so that in the ages to come He might show the surpassing riches of His grace in kindness toward us in Christ Jesus.

So while specific details of what follows the Millennium remain veiled, we can be certain that as that next chapter unfolds, we will be embarking on an infinite, wondrous journey, a story without end, a tale of glory and joy beyond our comprehension. As C.S. Lewis so eloquently concluded The Chronicles of Narnia,

> And for us this is the end of all stories, and we can most truly say that they all lived happily ever after. But for them it was only the beginning of the real story. All their life in this world and all their adventures in Narnia had only been the cover and the title page: now at last they were beginning Chapter One of the Great Story which no one on earth has read: which goes on forever: in which every chapter is better than the one before.[2]

Let us embrace this hope, the glorious anticipation of knowing that our future is secure in the hands of a loving and faithful God, whose plans for us are beyond anything we could ever ask or imagine (Ephesians. 3:20). Dwelling on this wonderful reality will nourish our souls, comfort us, and give us strength to endure the trials that we face.

Heaven and New Jerusalem

Chapter I

The Restoration of Earth

Throughout the last two thousand years, the church has wrestled with a profound question: What will God ultimately do with this earth? Will He utterly obliterate it, creating a completely new cosmos? Or will He, in His infinite power, redeem and restore this very earth to its original, Edenic splendor? This isn't a theological side-note; it strikes at the heart of our understanding of redemption and Heaven itself. How we interpret the Bible's prophetic glimpses of the eternal state hinges significantly on this crucial point.

Those who believe in the earth's annihilation often build their case on several key arguments. First, they point to the language of "newness" that Scripture employs when describing the future heavens and earth. We read of a "new heavens and new earth" in Isaiah (65:17, 66:22), 2 Peter (3:13), and Revelation (21:1). This emphasis on "new" suggests to some a complete and utter replacement. Second, they highlight the many biblical passages that speak of the present heavens and earth "passing away" or "perishing." From the Psalms (102:25-26) to the Gospels

Heaven and New Jerusalem

(Matthew 24:35, Luke 21:33), the Epistles (1 John 2:17), and Revelation (21:1), this theme of the death of the earth is prevalent.

Finally, they draw attention to certain passages that, on the surface, seem to depict the earth's total annihilation. One such verse that they reference, Isaiah 24:20, states: "The earth reels to and fro like a drunkard and it totters like a shack, for its transgression is heavy upon it, and it will fall, never to rise again." And Peter, in his second letter, describes a fiery end:

> But by His word the present heavens and earth are being reserved for fire, kept for the day of judgment and destruction of ungodly men… But the day of the Lord will come like a thief, in which the heavens will pass away with a roar and the elements will be destroyed with intense heat, and the earth and its works will be burned up. Since all these things are to be destroyed in this way, what sort of people ought you to be in holy conduct and godliness, looking for and hastening the coming of the day of God, because of which the heavens will be destroyed by burning, and the elements will melt with intense heat! But according to His promise we are looking for new heavens and a new earth, in which righteousness dwells. (2 Peter 3:7, 10-13).

On the other hand, consider Ecclesiastes 1:4: "A generation goes and a generation comes, but the earth remains forever." This speaks to the earth's enduring existence despite the ebb and flow of

Heaven and New Jerusalem

humanity. Similarly, Psalm 78:69 declares, "And He built His sanctuary like the heights, like the earth which He has founded forever." Here, the earth is presented as a foundation, a stable and lasting creation established by God Himself. Furthermore, Jesus, in Matthew 19:28, uses the phrase "in the regeneration" to describe the era of His reign. This word carries the weight of renewal, a rebirth, suggesting not annihilation, but a transformation back to something glorious. Peter, in Acts 3:19-21, speaks of a "period of restoration of all things," a time of refreshing that comes from the Lord, tied to Jesus' return.

So, how do we reconcile these seemingly disparate voices within Scripture? How do we hold together the verses that speak of the earth's passing away with those that affirm its enduring existence and future restoration? This tension is vital to grapple with. It forces us to dig deeper into God's redemptive plan. Is it possible that the "newness" Scripture speaks of involves a renewed and transformed oldness, a redemption of what was lost, rather than a complete replacement? Could the "passing away" be a purification, a refining fire that prepares the earth for its ultimate glory?

The key to understanding this tension in the Scriptures is Romans 8:18-23, which asserts,

> For I consider that the sufferings of this present time are not worthy to be compared with the glory that is to be revealed to us. For the anxious longing of the creation waits eagerly for the revealing of the sons of God. For the creation was subjected to futility, not willingly, but because of Him who subjected it, in hope that the creation itself also will be set free from its slavery to corruption into the freedom of the glory of the children of God. For we know that the whole creation groans and suffers the pains of childbirth together until now. And not only this, but also we ourselves, having the first fruits of the Spirit, even we ourselves groan within ourselves, waiting eagerly for our adoption as sons, the redemption of our body.

Heaven and New Jerusalem

If the very fabric of this world is destined to vanish, to be utterly erased, then why does it resonate with such a yearning groan, a desperate cry for the unveiling of God's children? Surely, if destruction was connected to the revelation of the children of God, this would not be the hope of creation. Picture a woman, her body wracked with the intense, searing pain of childbirth. Does she cry out for the annihilation of all things? Does she yearn for the extinguishing of her own existence? No! She endures, her spirit ablaze with the anticipation of the child she is about to hold, the joy that will eclipse all the pain. Similarly, creation's groan is not a death-wish, but a labor pang, a desperate yearning for the day of our resurrection. This is the moment when the chains of decay, the shackles of corruption, are finally shattered. It is the day when creation, too, will experience its own liberation and its own glorious redemption.

The miseries we endure and the trials we face are but fleeting moments compared to the radiant, immeasurable glory that awaits us in our resurrected state. This same truth echoes throughout the cosmos. Creation's present groaning and its current state of decay is utterly dwarfed by the magnificent dawn of its coming glory, a glory inextricably linked to our own.

Just as our own mortal frames are destined to return to dust, so too, in a very real sense, this present creation will fade and pass away, as the Scriptures themselves attest. Yet, this is not the final

Heaven and New Jerusalem

act! For just as we are promised a resurrection, a restoration to a glorified state, so too creation awaits its own regeneration, its own renewal, a "new heavens and a new earth," as promised. Think of it: the same principle that governs our own resurrection applies to the cosmos.

Consider our Lord Jesus, the firstfruits of those who rise. The very body that was broken, that perished on the cross, was raised from the tomb. The empty tomb, the nail-pierced hands, the spear-marked side—these were not illusions. They were the marks of the same Jesus, the same physical body and person, now gloriously transformed. Those who knew Him recognized Him, because He was the same Jesus, possessing the same body and composed of the same matter, yet utterly transformed and glorified.

This is the pattern for our own resurrection. As Philippians 3:21 and 1 Corinthians 15 so clearly declare, our resurrected bodies will be fashioned like His. We will be the same people, yet gloriously renewed. So it will also be with creation. Though it will pass away in its present form, it will be raised, restored, and regenerated, just as we will be. The very matter of this world, now groaning under the weight of corruption, will be made new.

Let's peer deeper into the verses that, at first blush, seem to speak of cosmic annihilation. Peter, in his inspired writing, speaks of the present heavens and earth passing away with a mighty roar, a fiery judgment that penetrates to the very core of its elemental makeup. This imagery, powerful and intense, might lead one to envision complete destruction. Yet consider the analogy of cremation. The body, reduced to ashes by fire, is not lost to eternity. Rather, it is the very same matter and the very same essence that someday will be resurrected and glorified. Likewise, our Lord Jesus, in His glorious resurrection, did not receive a completely new body, disconnected from the one that was broken and buried. His was the same body with the same scars, transformed, and glorified. So it shall be with us, and so it shall be with creation itself.

It is vital to recall Peter's earlier reference to the Flood (2 Peter 3:6). He points to this cataclysmic event as a precedent, a guarantee of God's coming judgment by fire. The Flood, he reminds us, "destroyed" the earth. A complete, world-encompassing inundation, it purged the earth of wickedness, radically altering its landscape, climate, and environment. Every inch of the earth was affected. Yet, was the earth annihilated? No! The earth we inhabit today is the very same earth that existed before the Flood. The destruction was transformative, not obliterative. The waters cleansed and reshaped, but they did not erase. In the same way, the coming fire, though far more intense, will not result in annihilation. It will be a purifying fire, a refining fire, a fire that transforms the very elements. Just as the Flood radically altered the earth, so too will this fiery judgment. But the essence, the substance of creation, will endure, to be resurrected and glorified, just as our own bodies will be.

The prophet Isaiah gives a stark declaration in Isaiah 24:20, where he declares that the earth will be judged and "will fall, never to rise again." But we should not rush to interpret this as a statement of utter, irreversible extinction. Rather, consider the weight of judgment being described. This is not a casual blow, but a devastating smiting, an overwhelming force that leaves the earth utterly incapable of self-restoration. The language here speaks of a profound, incapacitating defeat. Think of a historical parallel. One might say of the Austro-Hungarian Empire, which was defeated in World War I and collapsed, "The Austro-Hungarian Empire was dealt a death blow. It fell, never to rise again." This statement conveys the utter and complete defeat of a power, a regime so thoroughly crushed that it could not, by its own strength, recover.

Heaven and New Jerusalem

Similarly, Isaiah's words convey the magnitude of God's judgment upon the earth. The earth, reeling and swaying, is struck with such force that it cannot, on its own, lift itself from the dust. It is a death blow, a judgment so complete that the earth, left to its own devices, could not heal itself and could not return to its former state. However, let us not forget the power of our God, the Lord of resurrection and restoration. What is impossible for man and creation, is possible for Him. Though the earth will fall, unable to rise by its own power, God, in His infinite mercy and power, can and will resurrect it, transforming it into a new creation, a glorious testament to His redemptive power.

God's propensity for redemption casts a radiant light upon our understanding of Heaven, illuminating the nature of the new earth. Those prophecies that speak of a renewed creation are not referring to some ethereal realm disconnected from anything familiar, but to this very earth, resurrected and glorified, mirroring the transformation of our own bodies.

Moreover, the resurrected nations that will inhabit the new earth (Revelation 7:9, 21:24, and 22:2) are the very same nations that once walked this earth, now redeemed, restored, and inhabiting a world made new. But who are these nations and who comprises their ranks? Revelation 7:9 reveals a multitude, a vast throng of immortal, resurrected saints, gathered from every tribe, every tongue, and every people. Even those nations that perished before the gospel's reach will be represented, if only by the resurrected infants and children (including the pre-born) who were taken from them. And through God's sovereign protection, some mortals, those who stood firm against the Antichrist, will survive the Day of the Lord, as Isaiah 66:19 and Zechariah 14:16 affirm.

Furthermore, the prophetic passages hint at a remarkable continuity, a preservation of the geographic locations that these nations will inhabit. Acts 17:26 speaks of God assigning the boundaries of nations, and it appears that God will place people from the nations in their native homelands when He creates the new earth. Consider Isaiah 19, which foretells God's blessings upon Egypt and Assyria. A highway, a tangible connection, will unite these nations with Israel, suggesting they occupy their historic lands. If Egypt were relocated to modern-day Canada, and Assyria to Australia, such a highway would be nonsensical. Logic dictates that these nations will reside in their historic lands. Imagine the joy and the wonder as resurrected Assyrian and Egyptian saints reign over their nations, fulfilling the promise of Revelation 2:26-27.

And what of those nations that completely vanished, consumed by holocaust or assimilation, like ancient Babylon, long before the return of Jesus? It seems likely that resurrected saints from these lost nations will be granted lands within their ancestral homelands, coexisting peacefully with those who most recently

Heaven and New Jerusalem

have inhabited those regions. The new earth will be a place of restoration, a testament to God's mercy, where all things are made right.

We can, with confident expectation, anticipate that all that was good, all that was beautiful, and all that reflected the Creator's heart in this present earth will find its place, glorified and perfected, in the new earth. Though the mountains, even the majestic Grand Teton, will be leveled in the cataclysmic events of the last days (Revelation 16:20), this destruction will not be permanent. Grand Teton, a testament to God's artistry, a feature of the earth He deemed good, will surely rise again, transformed, its beauty enhanced beyond our wildest imaginations. Imagine the resurrected saints of the Shoshone nation dwelling upon its slopes and within its valleys, their ancestral home, alongside the resurrected saints of the American nation who once called Wyoming their own. They will live in harmony and perfect

fellowship, fulfilling the original purpose for which God created them, a purpose marred by the Fall, but now gloriously restored.

On that day, every nation and every people group that God has ever brought into being will experience the boundless blessings of His grace. As Isaiah 19:25 proclaims, "Blessed is Egypt My people, and Assyria the work of My hands, and Israel My inheritance," so too, we can anticipate a chorus of similar pronouncements. Surely, the same God who declared these blessings, the God who fashioned all nations for His glory, will also declare, "Blessed be the Shoshone my people, and America the work of my hands!" And so it will be for every people, every tribe, and every nation, a testament to God's redemptive power, His unwavering love, and His glorious plan to restore all things.

Once again, C.S. Lewis' *The Chronicles of Narnia* provides an excellent portrayal of what Heaven will look like with his description of the *real* Narnia which the Pevensie children encountered at the end of the story:

> "Why!" exclaimed Peter. "It's England. And that's the house itself—Professor Kirk's old home in the country where all our adventures began!"
>
> "I thought that house had been destroyed," said Edmund.
>
> "So it was," said the Faun. "But you are now looking at the England within England, the real England

Heaven and New Jerusalem

just as this is the real Narnia. And in that inner England no good thing is destroyed."[3]

Chapter II

The Presence of the Saints on Earth During the Millennium

There is a belief that robs many Christians of the hope of Christ's promised reign: that believers will be absent from the earth during the Millennial Kingdom, sequestered in some distant celestial realm, while our Lord Jesus rules here below. This is a somber and frankly, unbiblical concept. This idea stems from a misinterpretation of Revelation 20:4-5, which says,

> Then I saw thrones, and they sat on them, and judgment was given to them. And I saw the souls of those who had been beheaded because of their testimony of Jesus and because of the word of God, and those who had not worshiped the beast or his image, and had not received the mark on their forehead and on their hand; and they came to life and reigned with Christ for a thousand years. The rest of the dead did not come to life until the thousand years were completed.

Many, upon reading these verses, hastily conclude that "the rest of the dead" refers to all Christians who have passed away, save for those martyred by the Antichrist. They imagine a scenario where the Antichrist's victims reign with Christ, while other believers remain in Heaven until the Millennium's end. But this interpretation crumbles under the weight of scriptural truth. 2 Thessalonians 2:1-5 unequivocally states that the resurrection and rapture of *all* believers occurs before the Day of the Lord, which marks the commencement of the Millennium. All Christians who have died previous to the beginning of the Millennium will be raised at this time. Logically, then, "the rest of the dead" can only refer to unbelievers, those who remain in death until the thousand years are complete. They are the ones who will be raised to face judgment at the Great White Throne (Revelation 20:11-15), and ultimately, to be consigned to the Lake of Fire.

We must discern, as Scripture reveals, two distinct types of resurrections: the first resurrection, which is unto life, and the second resurrection, which is unto judgment and death, as John 5:29 so clearly states. The first type of resurrection was exemplified by our Lord Jesus Christ, the firstfruits of those who sleep (1 Corinthians 15:23). And, as Matthew 27:52 attests, it was also experienced by those saints who were raised from the dead at the moment of Jesus' crucifixion. While Scripture remains silent on their subsequent journey, I believe that they most likely ascended to Heaven, just as our Lord did after His glorious resurrection.

However, this first resurrection is not confined to the past. It will also be experienced in the future by the two witnesses of Revelation 11:11, and by all saints, living and asleep, who await

Heaven and New Jerusalem

the second coming of Christ. This includes those martyred by the Beast, and every other believer who has not yet been raised, as Matthew 24:31 and 1 Corinthians 15:23 confirm. Furthermore, 1 Corinthians 15:24 hints at another glorious resurrection at the close of the Millennium. This, it seems, will be the transformation of mortal saints who lived through the thousand-year reign. They will be changed,  given immortal bodies, just as those alive at Christ's second coming will be transformed in the twinkling of an eye.

    A diligent reading of Revelation 20 does not restrict the resurrection to those martyred by the Antichrist. John does not declare that they alone were raised. Nor does he specify that their resurrection occurred after the Beast's defeat at Armageddon. Instead, John simply states that he *saw* the souls of those who were martyred by the Antichrist and that they came to life. While their martyrdom at the hands of the Beast and their subsequent resurrection are certain, the timing of their raising is not explicitly stated. It seems John, having just received a vision of the

Antichrist's downfall in Revelation 19, is given another vision which highlights the contrast: the Beast's total defeat versus the saints' victory, even in death. He emphasizes that those whom the Antichrist sought to destroy, those whom he murdered, ultimately triumphed.

Now, consider the second type of resurrection, described later in Revelation 20. This resurrection, a resurrection unto death, as far as we are aware, is a singular event, occurring only once at the close of the Millennium. It is the raising of the wicked, those who have rejected God throughout the entirety of history, to stand before the Great White Throne and face judgment for their sins. They are sentenced to the second death, the Lake of Fire (Revelation 20:11-15). Therefore, when John speaks of "the rest of the dead" in Revelation 20:5, he is clearly referring to these wicked individuals, those who are raised in the second resurrection at the end of the Millennium.

Not only is Revelation 20 misunderstood by many Christians here, but there are many passages of Scripture which directly contradict this idea. Consider 1 Thessalonians 3:12-13, which pronounces,

> And may the Lord cause you to increase and abound in love for one another, and for all people, just as we also do for you; so that He may establish your hearts without blame

Heaven and New Jerusalem

in holiness before our God and Father at the coming of our Lord Jesus with all His saints.

The words of Paul, inspired by the Spirit, declare that Jesus will return with *all* His saints, every believer who has ever lived, up to that very moment. There is no separation and no exclusion.

And what of the rapture, that blessed hope? 1 Thessalonians 4:16-17 gives even more detail:

> For the Lord Himself will descend from heaven with a shout, with the voice of the archangel and with the trumpet of God, and the dead in Christ will rise first. Then we who are alive and remain will be caught up together with them in the clouds to meet the Lord in the air, and so we shall always be with the Lord.

Heaven and New Jerusalem

From that moment onward, from the very instant of the rapture, we are *always* with the Lord, united with all the saints in our resurrected bodies. Whether we are among those alive at the end or those raised from the dead, we are forever joined with Him and with our brothers and sisters. Let us banish the notion that we will be separated from our Lord during His earthly reign. If He is in the clouds, we are in the clouds with Him. If He reigns upon the earth, we reign upon the earth with Him, as 2 Timothy 2:12 affirms. There is no division, separation, partiality, or segregation, only the glorious unity of Christ and His saints, forever and ever.

With this in mind, the account of the marriage feast for Christ and the Church and the Lord's return with the armies of Heaven, described in Revelation 19:6-16, takes on an even more magnificent dimension:

> Then I heard something like the voice of a great multitude and like the sound of many waters and like the sound of mighty peals of thunder, saying, "Hallelujah! For the Lord our God, the Almighty, reigns. Let us rejoice and be glad and give the glory to Him, for the marriage of the Lamb has come and His bride has made herself ready." It was given to her to clothe herself in fine linen, bright and clean; for the fine linen is the righteous acts of the saints. Then he said to me, "Write, 'Blessed are those who are invited to the marriage supper of the Lamb.'" And he said to me,

Heaven and New Jerusalem

"These are true words of God"... And I saw heaven opened, and behold, a white horse, and He who sat on it is called Faithful and True, and in righteousness He judges and wages war. His eyes are a flame of fire, and on His head are many diadems; and He has a name written on Him which no one knows except Himself. He is clothed with a robe dipped in blood, and His name is called The Word of God. And the armies which are in heaven, clothed in fine linen, white and clean, were following Him on white horses. From His mouth comes a sharp sword, so that with it He may strike down the nations, and He will rule them with a rod of iron; and He treads the wine press of the fierce wrath of God, the Almighty. And on His robe and on His thigh He has a name written, "King of kings, and Lord of lords."

Here, we see the King of kings returning, followed by "the armies which were in heaven." Many assume these armies are solely composed of angelic beings, and indeed, 2 Thessalonians 1:6-8 assures us that angels will be present. But a closer look reveals a deeper truth. These armies are described as being clothed in "fine linen, white and clean." Does that sound familiar? It should! Just a few verses earlier, the same phrase is used to describe the garments of the saints, the Bride of Christ, invited to the marriage supper of the Lamb. This parallel strongly indicates

Heaven and New Jerusalem

that the armies of Heaven are not just angels, but the redeemed saints of God, returning with their Lord.

And consider the "rod of iron" with which Jesus will rule the nations. This same phrase is used in Revelation 2:26-27, where those who overcome are promised authority over the nations: "He who overcomes, and he who keeps My deeds until the end, to him I will give authority over the nations; and he shall rule them with a rod of iron, as the vessels of the potter are broken to pieces, as I also have received authority from My Father." Do you see the connection? The saints, the overcomers, will share in Christ's rule.

Heaven and New Jerusalem

This means that the armies of Heaven, in their fine linen, are not mere spectators. They are active participants in Christ's victory and in His righteous reign.

It's a staggering truth, isn't it? If you have placed your faith in Jesus, no matter how great or small you are in this life, you—yes, you!—will be part of this glorious, heavenly army. You will return with the King of kings, and you will share in His dominion over the nations. Colossians 3:4 beautifully summarizes this hope: "When Christ, who is our life, is revealed, then you also will be revealed with Him in glory."

Chapter III

The Descent of New Jerusalem at the Beginning of the Millennium

Revelation 21-22 speaks of the creation of the new heavens and earth and the descent of New Jerusalem, God's Holy City. Although Christians rightly look to this passage for details about their eternal home, it is a commonly-held belief that these chapters describe events which occur *after* the conclusion of Christ's thousand year reign on earth. This interpretation raises troubling questions, particularly when we grapple with Old Testament prophecies. Isaiah 65:17 and 20, for instance, speak of the new heavens and earth, yet they also mention death still occurring for a limited time. This isn't consistent with the time after the end of the Millennium, when death will be abolished completely (1 Corinthians 15:26).

Furthermore, the striking similarities between the descriptions of the new heavens and earth in Revelation 21-22 and the prophecies concerning the Millennial Reign in the Old Testament, especially those found in Isaiah and Ezekiel, cannot be ignored. Some Old Testament prophecies appear to almost be quoted verbatim in Revelation 21-22, strongly suggesting that they are referring to the same period of time. Unless we consider the possibility of New Jerusalem's descent occurring at the beginning of the Millennium, these discrepancies become exceedingly difficult to reconcile.

The timing of these events profoundly impacts our understanding of biblical prophecy, particularly concerning Heaven and New Jerusalem. If the new heavens and earth are established at the end of the Millennium, then the vast majority of Old Testament prophecies regarding the future would apply exclusively to the Millennial Reign, leaving us with a very limited understanding of Heaven itself. Therefore, in our pursuit of truth and in our study of Heaven and New Jerusalem, it is imperative that we carefully examine the timing of these events to understand the full scope of what God has in store for us in the future. After careful examination of God's Word, I find it more probable than not that the new heavens and earth are created and New Jerusalem descends at the *beginning* of the Millennium, rather than the end. However, I understand why many Christians hesitate to embrace this view. There are two primary stumbling blocks.

First, the placement of Revelation 21-22 after Revelation 20, which describes the Millennium, naturally leads to the assumption that these chapters describe events that follow the Millennium. However, we must remember that, while Revelation is generally chronological, it is not arranged in strict linear order. It is a book of interwoven narratives, sometimes presented out of

Heaven and New Jerusalem

sequence. Each narrative must be studied in relation to others to discover its proper place within the overall picture. Furthermore, some narratives offer a broad overview of a time period, while others provide a more detailed, "zoomed-in" perspective. Consider, for example, Revelation 6, which offers a summary of the birth pangs and the Great Tribulation, briefly mentioning the martyrdom of the saints in verses 9-11. Chapters 12-13 then "zoom in," giving us a more detailed account of the Beast's rise and the specific reasons for the saints' persecution. It is likely that the same principle applies to Revelation 20 and 21-22. Chapter 20 provides a broad, summarized view of the entire Millennial period, from beginning to end. Chapters 21-22 then "zoom in," offering a more detailed, expanded view of the new earth, New Jerusalem, and daily life in the Millennial Kingdom.

Heaven and New Jerusalem

Now, let us address the second stumbling block, an emotional hurdle that many face when considering the idea of death persisting, even for a time, in the new heavens and earth. It is understandable that this concept causes unease, even distress. Yet, we must anchor our understanding in the unwavering truth of God's Word. Let us remember that even with New Jerusalem arriving at the Millennium's dawn, death will not go on forever. Its final defeat remains firmly fixed at the end of that glorious thousand-year reign. 1 Corinthians 15:22-26 provides unshakeable clarity:

> For as in Adam all die, so also in Christ all will be made alive. But each in his own order: Christ the first fruits, after that those who are Christ's at His coming, then comes the end, when He hands over the kingdom to the God and Father, when He has abolished all rule and all authority and power. For He must reign until He has put all His enemies under His feet. The last enemy that will be abolished is death.

Regardless of when we believe New Jerusalem descends, this passage plainly states that death's ultimate eradication will not occur until Christ has subdued all His enemies, which will not happen until the Millennium's conclusion, after Satan's brief release and final rebellion. Then, when Christ's mission is fully accomplished, God will utterly abolish death from all Creation and

Heaven and New Jerusalem

will prepare a magnificent banquet for all peoples (Isaiah 25:6-9). We cannot allow our emotions to overshadow the clear pronouncements of Scripture. The persistence of death for a brief time in the Millennium does not diminish the ultimate triumph of Christ. God's plan unfolds in its perfect timing, and His promises are sure. Death, the last enemy, will be vanquished, and Christ will reign supreme.

It is also vital to remember that, after Christ returns, death will have no dominion over the resurrected saints ever again. Revelation 21:2-4 paints a breathtaking picture:

> And I saw the holy city, new Jerusalem, coming down out of heaven from God, made ready as a bride adorned for her husband. And I heard a loud voice from the throne, saying, "Behold, the tabernacle of God is among men, and He will dwell among them, and they shall be His people, and God Himself will be among them, and He will wipe away every tear from their eyes; and there will no longer be any death;

there will no longer be any mourning, or crying, or pain; the first things have passed away."

Let us now examine the scriptural evidence that supports the descent of New Jerusalem at the dawn of the Millennium. We will consider the relevant verses in Revelation 21-22, drawing connections to the Old Testament prophecies of the Millennial Reign, and addressing any apparent contradictions. In so doing, we will also learn a lot about New Jerusalem, in all its glorious detail.

Revelation 21:1 sets the stage: "Then I saw a new heaven and a new earth; for the first heaven and the first earth passed away, and there is no longer any sea." Now, recall Isaiah 65:17, which begins a prophecy concerning the Millennium, and also speaks of a "new heavens and a new earth." Is it not highly improbable that these two passages refer to different events? Surely, the Jewish Christians who first encountered John's vision

would have immediately recognized the connection to Isaiah's familiar prophecy.

But then we encounter the phrase, "and there is no longer any sea." At first, this seems to contradict Old Testament prophecies, such as Isaiah 60:5 and Ezekiel 47:8, 10, 15, and 17-20, which speak of seas during the Millennium. How do we reconcile this? The key lies in the preceding phrase, "for the first heaven and the first earth passed away."

When the first heaven and earth will be judged, the sea, too, will perish. Revelation 16:3 tells us that the sea's waters will turn to blood, and every sea creature will die. John, who witnessed this, could rightly declare, "there is no longer any sea." However, although the sea will perish with the old earth, this does not mean that it will not be raised up with the new earth. Indeed, in the new heaven and new earth, God will recreate the sea. Ezekiel 47:1-12 and Zechariah 14:8 reveal that the river of life, flowing from God's throne, will transform the sea into freshwater. And it is likely that God will cause the resurrected sea creatures to adapt to this change and thrive in this new environment.

We must understand that the absence of the sea in Revelation 21:1 is a description of the judgment of the first creation, not a denial of the sea's existence in the new creation. God's creative power is not limited; He can and will restore all things, bringing forth a new heaven and a new earth, where both

Heaven and New Jerusalem

land and sea reflect His glory and the original, good Edenic purpose that He made them for.

Next, Revelation 21:2 says, "And I saw the holy city, new Jerusalem, coming down out of heaven from God, made ready as a bride adorned for her husband." This image, so radiant and full of promise, echoes the very heart of Old Testament prophecy. Immediately following his declaration of the new heavens and new earth, Isaiah 65:18 proclaims, "But be glad and rejoice forever in what I create; for behold, I create Jerusalem for rejoicing." Moreover, consider Isaiah 62:4, a passage that speaks of Millennial New Jerusalem:

> It will no longer be said to you, "Forsaken," nor to your land will it any longer be said, "Desolate"; but you will be called, "My delight is in her," and your land, "Married"; for the LORD delights in you, and to Him your land will be married.

In Revelation 21:3, John hears a resounding voice from the throne, saying, "Behold, the tabernacle of God is among men, and He will dwell among them, and they shall be His people, and God Himself will be among them." Ezekiel 37:27, a prophecy about Millennial Israel, echoes this divine promise: "My dwelling place also will be with them; and I will be their God, and they will be My people." Moreover, Zechariah 2:10-11 further amplifies this truth:

Heaven and New Jerusalem

"Sing for joy and be glad, O daughter of Zion; for behold I am coming and I will dwell in your midst," declares the LORD. "Many nations will join themselves to the LORD in that day and will become My people. Then I will dwell in your midst, and you will know that the LORD of hosts has sent Me to you."

Furthermore, Ezekiel 48:35, speaking of the city of Jerusalem during the Millennium, declares, "And the name of the city from that day shall be, 'The LORD is there.'" The dwelling of God among men, the gathering of nations, the intimate communion between Creator and creation—these are the hallmarks of the Millennial Reign, and they are precisely what John witnesses in Revelation 21:3.

Revelation 21:4, which was quoted a few paragraphs ago, says almost the exact same thing as Isaiah 65:19, which remarks, "I will also rejoice in Jerusalem and be glad in My people; and there will no longer be heard in her the voice of weeping and the sound of crying." Isaiah 65:17 clearly identifies this passage as addressing the new heavens and earth, but immediately after Isaiah speaks of a cessation of sorrow, he acknowledges the presence of death (Isaiah 65:17), which continues in the Millennium. Any wicked mortals who rebel against God and who stay outside the city will still experience death, mourning, crying, and pain (Isaiah 65:20 and Revelation 20:8-9 and 22:15). These are the

Heaven and New Jerusalem

consequences of rejecting God's grace and the bitter fruit of unrepentance. The contrast is stark: within the city among the saints, eternal life, joy, and peace; outside, the lingering shadows of a fallen world. Yet, even these shadows will ultimately be dispelled, when Christ's reign is complete and his work of restoration has, in totality, made all things new.

In Revelation 21:9, John is approached by "one of the seven angels who had the seven bowls full of the seven last plagues" who declares, "Come here, I will show you the bride, the wife of the Lamb." First, let us not overlook the language used to describe New Jerusalem. "The bride, the wife of the Lamb"—a phrase reminiscent of Isaiah 62:4, a passage we explored earlier. There, too, New Jerusalem is spoken of in terms of marriage, as the wife of God.

Second, the identity of this angel which spoke to John, one who had participated in the pouring out of God's wrath, is worthy of our consideration. Could this be a mere coincidence? Or does it hint at a temporal connection, a proximity between the outpouring of judgment and the descent of New Jerusalem? While it is possible that this angel is showing John a vision of events a thousand years distant, it seems more likely that the angel is revealing to John something that happens soon after the bowls of wrath were poured out.

Heaven and New Jerusalem

Continuing, Revelation 21:10 comments, "And he carried me away in the Spirit to a great and high mountain, and showed me the holy city, Jerusalem, coming down out of heaven from God..." Likewise, Ezekiel 40:2, which commences a prophecy concerning Millennial Israel, speaks of a remarkably similar experience, "In the visions of God He brought me into the land of Israel and set me on a very high mountain, and on it to the south there was a structure like a city."

In Revelation 21:11 and 18-21, John beholds a city,

...having the glory of God. Her brilliance was like a very costly stone, as a stone of crystal-clear jasper... The material of the wall was jasper; and the city was pure gold, like clear glass. The foundation stones of the city wall were adorned with every kind of precious stone. The first foundation stone was jasper; the second, sapphire; the third, chalcedony; the fourth, emerald; the fifth, sardonyx; the sixth, sardius; the seventh, chrysolite; the eighth, beryl; the ninth, topaz; the tenth, chrysoprase; the eleventh, jacinth;

the twelfth, amethyst. And the twelve gates were twelve pearls; each one of the gates was a single pearl.

These descriptions echo the prophetic pronouncements of Isaiah 54:11-12, a passage that speaks of Millennial Jerusalem:

O afflicted one, storm-tossed, and not comforted, behold, I will set your stones in antimony, and your foundations I will lay in sapphires. Moreover, I will make your battlements of rubies, and your gates of crystal, and your entire wall of precious stones.

Some might point to a perceived discrepancy: John describes the gates as being made of pearl, while Isaiah speaks of gates of crystal. But let us not be hasty in drawing conclusions. Is it not possible that the gatehouse itself is formed of a single, magnificent pearl, while the bars or framework of the gate are composed of crystal? Or perhaps vice versa? This would just be one simple way to reconcile these descriptions. But it is important not to lose sight of the incredible similarity between these two visions of the jewel-encrusted city of New Jerusalem.

The similarities become more apparent in other passages. Revelation 21:12-13 mentions that New Jerusalem,

…had a great and high wall, with twelve gates, and at the gates twelve angels; and names were written on them, which are the names of the twelve tribes of the sons of Israel. There were three gates on the east and three gates on

Heaven and New Jerusalem

the north and three gates on the south and three gates on the west.

Ezekiel 48:30-34 gives the exact same details:

These are the exits of the city: on the north side... shall be the gates of the city, named for the tribes of Israel, three gates toward the north: the gate of Reuben, one; the gate of Judah, one; the gate of Levi, one. On the east side... shall be three gates: the gate of Joseph, one; the gate of Benjamin, one; the gate of Dan, one. On the south side... shall be three gates: the gate of Simeon, one; the gate of Issachar, one; the gate of Zebulun, one. On the west side... shall be three gates: the gate of Gad, one; the gate of Asher, one; the gate of Naphtali, one.

Heaven and New Jerusalem

In Revelation 21:15-16, John witnesses an angel with,

...a gold measuring rod to measure the city, and its gates and its wall. The city is laid out as a square, and its length is as great as the width; and he measured the city with the rod, fifteen hundred miles; its length and width and height are equal.

Here we encounter a point of confusion for many. John recorded what he witnessed using the common measurements of his day. Some translations, seeking to simplify, approximate 12,000 stadia to 1,500 miles. While the translators interpreted this text in this manner in an attempt to make this passage more understandable, it is crucial to remember that John's original text specifies 12,000 stadia as the length of the measurement.

Furthermore, many Western readers assume that New Jerusalem's length, width, and height are each 12,000 stadia. However, a careful reading of the text reveals a different picture. The text states that only the length and width (not the height) are 12,000 stadia, and it appears this is the measurement of the *area* of the length and width, not the individual dimensions of the length and width. This indicates that the actual length, width, and height (which are all equal) would each be approximately 109.5 stadia.

The length of a stadia varied in ancient times, falling within an estimated range of 149 meters (0.093 miles) to 298 meters (0.185 miles).[4] For instance, Eratosthenes, a renowned Greek

Heaven and New Jerusalem

mathematician, used a stadia of 166.7 meters (0.1036 miles).⁵ Although we don't for sure how long the stadias were that the angel used to measure New Jerusalem, if we use Eratosthenes' stadia as an example, the length, width, and height of New Jerusalem would each be approximately 11.34 miles.

This is still an unbelievably monumental size, which few can accurately envision. Imagine the Burj Khalifa, which is currently the tallest building in our world at a mere half-mile high. New Jerusalem, at a height of eleven miles, is taller than the Burj Khalifa by more than twenty-two times! Also consider Mount Everest, that majestic peak that reaches nearly six miles into the sky. New Jerusalem would dwarf it, rising almost twice as high. Even the cruising altitude of a commercial airliner, typically around six or seven

miles above sea level, pales in comparison to the pinnacle of this celestial city. The vast majority of humanity, even those who have flown, have never come close to approaching the heights of New Jerusalem.

Next, we must analyze the measurements of Millennial Jerusalem as revealed in Ezekiel 45:6 and 48:30-34. Here, we find another city laid out in a square, much like the New Jerusalem we have just explored. However, a curious detail emerges: while the measurements for each side of the square are given as 4,500 or, including its border, 5,000, the original Hebrew text provides no specific unit of measurement. Context, as always, is paramount. Ezekiel, in chapters 40-48, consistently employs either cubits or rods as units of measure. Thus, it is almost certain that one of these two units is implied in the measurements of the city that Ezekiel recorded. Translations, recognizing this, often assume one of these units, adding them in italics, signifying that it is an interpretive addition, a best guess based on the context. But why did Ezekiel omit the unit? Just as we might say, "I am six three," and be understood to mean "six feet, three inches," so too, Ezekiel relied on his audience's recognition of implied measurements.

Which unit was implied? Rod, I believe, is the more probable choice. The Temple complex, described in Ezekiel 45:2 as "five hundred by five hundred," likely used rods as its implied unit. This is supported by the fact that smaller features within the

Temple are specifically measured in cubits (see Ezekiel 42:8), suggesting a deliberate contrast. Because of this, if the city were measured in cubits, it would be only slightly larger than the Temple complex, which is an unlikely scenario. It makes far more sense that both the Temple and the city would be measured using the same implied unit, and that the city would be significantly larger than the Temple.

So how long is a rod? Widely accepted as six cubits in length, the rod's precise measurement, like the cubit itself, varied across societies and time periods. The cubit, being the distance between a human elbow and middle finger, naturally fluctuated. Henry Sulley, a nineteenth-century British engineer and commentator on Ezekiel 40-48, estimated the rod's length to be between 10.5 feet and 12 feet.[6] This range allows us to calculate the city's size. Including the 500 rod border surrounding the city's 4,500 rod walls (Ezekiel 45:6), we arrive at a total city size of 5,000 rods per side. Using Sulley's estimates, the city's dimensions would fall between 9.94 miles (minimum) and 11.36 miles (maximum) per side. Astonishingly, the upper range of this estimate nearly perfectly aligns with New Jerusalem's dimensions that we calculated earlier from John's vision. While the exact sizes of the rod and stadia remain uncertain, this convergence proves their compatibility and their harmonious witness to God's plan.

Heaven and New Jerusalem

Sulley himself concluded that Ezekiel's city was approximately 11 miles long and wide, expressing his amazement at this magnificent revelation:

> Our wonder increases when we consider the detailed arrangements of the third section of the holy square. A city and its suburbs, over eleven miles each way, is probably larger than any city of this Gentile era, except London.[7]

Imagine a jewel-encrusted, golden city, 11 miles wide, long, and high! A marvel of architecture, surpassing any human creation, a dwelling place of unparalleled glory. It will be the greatest architectural wonder in human history and will be an incredible place to live.

What form will this city take? Is it a perfect cube, a symmetrical marvel? Or might it be a pyramid, a structure with rooms and buildings nestled within its ascending levels? After all, Jesus tells us in John 14:2-3 that His Father's house has many rooms. If pyramid-shaped, this could explain the prophetic descriptions of the "mountain of the Lord," the home of God, found in Isaiah 2:2-3, Joel 3:17, Micah 4:1, and Zechariah 8:3. Or perhaps, New Jerusalem is a city with exposed buildings, its skyscrapers reaching heights of over ten miles, piercing the heavens themselves. Regardless of its precise form, New Jerusalem is a city of unimaginable grandeur, a dwelling place worthy of our God.

Heaven and New Jerusalem

Moving on, Revelation 21:22 adds, "I saw no temple in it [the city of New Jerusalem], for the Lord God the Almighty and the Lamb are its temple." This resonates with Ezekiel's vision of the Millennial Temple in Ezekiel 40-48, since the Temple is not in the city (Ezekiel 45:1-6).

Revelation 21:23 states, "And the city has no need of the sun or of the moon to shine on it, for the glory of God has illumined it, and its lamp is the Lamb" (also see Revelation 22:5). Isaiah 60:19, with nearly identical words, proclaims, "No longer will you have the sun for light by day, nor for brightness will the moon give you light; but you will have the LORD for an everlasting light, and your God for your glory."

Although commonly interpreted this way, these verses do not assert the cessation of the sun and moon's existence. In fact, Revelation 22:2 and Ezekiel 47:12 speak of the tree of life bearing fruit *monthly*, a clear indication of the moon's presence, as months are time measurements rooted in lunar cycles. These lunar phases, caused by the earth and moon's orbits, light, and the earth's shadow, also necessitate the existence of a sun that illuminates both earth and moon. However, within New Jerusalem, the lights will never dim and never fade. The glory of the Lord, the very presence of the Lamb, will provide an eternal, unwavering illumination. The city's inhabitants will have no need for the sun, the moon, or any artificial light source. This prophecy is not a

Heaven and New Jerusalem

denial of the continued existence of the sun and moon, but a revelation of God's surpassing glory. The sun and moon will continue their celestial dance, but within New Jerusalem, the light of God's presence will reign supreme, an eternal dawn that knows no sunset.

Now we will turn our focus to the gathering of the nations, the influx of glory into New Jerusalem, as revealed in Revelation 21:24-26, which says, "The nations will walk by its light, and the kings of the earth will bring their glory into it. In the daytime (for

Heaven and New Jerusalem

there will be no night there) its gates will never be closed; and they will bring the glory and the honor of the nations into it." Isaiah 60:3 proclaims, concerning Jerusalem during the Millennium, "Nations will come to your light, and kings to the brightness of your rising." Isaiah 62:2 further declares, "The nations will see your righteousness, and all kings your glory; and you will be called by a new name which the mouth of the LORD will designate."

The sameness of these visions, the shared language of nations and kings, of glory and honor, is unmistakable. New Jerusalem, as depicted by John, is not a separate entity, but the fulfillment of the prophecies spoken by Isaiah. The mention of a "new name" in Isaiah 62:2 is particularly noteworthy. Could this be a reference to the very name "New Jerusalem," as revealed in Revelation 21:2? It is an intriguing possibility. The nations walking in the light of the city, the kings bringing their glory—these are not allegories. They are glimpses into the reality of the Millennial Reign, a time when all nations will acknowledge the Lord's sovereignty, and His glory will fill the earth.

The river and trees of life, which are the very essence of God's restorative power, are revealed in Revelation 22:1-2:

> Then he showed me a river of the water of life, clear as crystal, coming from the throne of God and of the Lamb, in the middle of its street. On either side of the river was the tree of life, bearing twelve kinds of fruit, yielding its fruit

Heaven and New Jerusalem

every month; and the leaves of the tree were for the healing of the nations.

Ezekiel 47:12, with a striking parallel, proclaims,

By the river on its bank, on one side and on the other, will grow all kinds of trees for food. Their leaves will not wither and their fruit will not fail. They will bear every month because their water flows from the sanctuary, and their fruit will be for food and their leaves for healing.

The river of life, the trees bearing fruit monthly, the leaves for healing—these are not coincidental similarities. The consistency of these visions reinforce the unity of God's prophetic word.

Heaven and New Jerusalem

A seeming discrepancy may be seen in Revelation 22:3 and Ezekiel 43:7. Revelation declares, "...The throne of God and of the Lamb will be in it [the city]..." while Ezekiel proclaims, "Son of man, this [the Temple] is the place of My throne and the place of the soles of My feet, where I will dwell among the sons of Israel forever." How, some might ask, can God's throne reside in two distinct locations? Does this not create a contradiction?

It does not. Consider the history of earthly kings. It is not uncommon for a monarch to reign over multiple kingdoms and to possess multiple thrones, symbols of their authority over different realms. King George III, for instance, held thrones in both England and Hanover, since he was monarch over both nations. Is it then inconceivable that our God, the King of kings, could have multiple thrones? A throne within New Jerusalem, establishing His dominion over the entire earth, and a special throne within the Temple, signifying His particular kingship over Israel? There is no contradiction here. It is simply a reflection of God's multifaceted sovereignty. Furthermore, though Scripture does not explicitly state it, is it not possible that God could establish special thrones within every nation on earth? After all, all nations are His handiwork. Is He not King over each of them individually, as well as collectively? So, the establishment of the thrones of God in all nations certainly seems to be a possibility.

Heaven and New Jerusalem

Next, Revelation 22:6 states, "And he said to me, 'These words are faithful and true'; and the Lord, the God of the spirits of the prophets, sent His angel to show to His bond-servants the things which must soon take place." Notice the Lord's designation as "the God of the spirits of the prophets." This is not a random title, but a profound affirmation. John, in his inspired writing, draws our attention to the continuity of divine revelation and the unbroken chain of prophetic witness. Think of it: many prophets of old were granted glimpses of Millennial New Jerusalem, visions that resonate with what John himself beheld. It is as if John is saying, "The very God who revealed these truths to the prophets before me is the same God who guarantees their fulfillment in the future."

Consider the implications of this statement. If New Jerusalem's descent was relegated to the end of the Millennium, this phrase would seem strangely out of place, even nonsensical. In that scenario, John would be virtually alone in receiving significant prophecies about the new heavens and earth. The vast majority of detailed prophecies concerning the period after the tribulation period (known as Daniel's seventieth week), with only two or three exceptions in Isaiah, focus on the Millennial Reign. The emphasis on the phrase "God of the spirits of the prophets" makes far more sense if New Jerusalem descends at the beginning of the Millennium. It highlights the consistency of God's revelation and the harmony between Old and New Testament prophecies. It is a testament to the fact that the God who spoke through the prophets of old about this coming city is the same God who speaks through John, and the same God who will bring His promises to pass.

Lastly, let us turn our hearts to the closing invitation of this passage, the gracious call that echoes through the ages, as revealed in Revelation 22:17: "The Spirit and the bride say, 'Come.' And let the one who hears say, 'Come.' And let the one who is thirsty come; let the one who wishes take the water of life without cost." For Jewish readers, these words would have resonated deeply with the invitation found in Isaiah 55:1: "Ho! Every one who thirsts, come to the waters; and you who have no money come, buy and eat. Come, buy wine and milk without money and without cost." The language of thirst, of coming to the waters, of freely receiving

Heaven and New Jerusalem

the bounty of God's provision—these are not mere coincidences. The Spirit who invites us to "come" and enjoy God's goodness is the same Spirit who showed the prophets these glorious things that will soon come to pass.

As we have seen, the scriptural connections and parallels between Revelation's description of the new heaven and earth and the Old Testament prophecies about the Millennium are undeniable. Within the scriptural evidence, we find additional logical considerations that bolster this position.

Heaven and New Jerusalem

For instance, the Bible confirms that New Jerusalem already exists, even right now. Paul speaks of New Jerusalem in the present tense in Galatians 4:26 when he says, "But the Jerusalem above is free; she is our mother." Hebrews 12:22-24 further affirms this, stating plainly,

> But you have come to Mount Zion and to the city of the living God, the heavenly Jerusalem, and to myriads of angels, to the general assembly and church of the firstborn who are enrolled in heaven, and to God, the Judge of all, and to the spirits of the righteous made perfect, and to Jesus, the mediator of a new covenant, and to the sprinkled blood, which speaks better than the blood of Abel.

This heavenly Jerusalem, the abode of Jesus Himself and "the spirits of the righteous made perfect" is where believers go when they fall asleep in this present age. When this happens to us, Philippians 1:23 confirms that we are promised to be with Christ. In Chapter II, we established that all the inhabitants of Heaven will accompany Jesus when he returns to earth. Why, then, would New Jerusalem remain vacant and unoccupied in Heaven until the Millennium's end? Even God Himself will dwell on earth during the Millennium, as Ezekiel 37:26-27 and 48:35 declare. It is far more probable and more consistent with the grand narrative of Scripture that a complete and glorious invasion of earth by Heaven will occur at Christ's return. Every inhabitant and everything in

Heaven and New Jerusalem

Heaven, including the city of New Jerusalem itself, will descend with Him.

This is not a piecemeal arrival over a millennia, but a grand, unified event, a cosmic convergence of Heaven and earth, a glorious culmination of God's redemptive plan. New Jerusalem, already prepared and inhabited, will be the crown jewel of Christ's Millennial Reign, a testament to His victory and His eternal love.

To grasp the truth of New Jerusalem's descent at the Millennium's dawn is to unlock a treasure trove of understanding, a revelation that transforms our perspective on Heaven itself. It means that the vast and detailed prophecies of the Millennium found in the Old Testament are not merely descriptions of a

temporary earthly reign, but glimpses into the very nature of our eternal home, the Kingdom of Heaven, where Christ will reign forever. The realization that the Millennium's commencement may be imminent, perhaps a mere decade or two away, and that we, if we are in

Heaven and New Jerusalem

Christ, will reign with Him forever, should ignite within us a fervent desire to explore the writings of the Old Testament prophets.

When this truth first dawned upon me, I was consumed with a hunger to glean every detail and every nuance of their prophetic pronouncements. God, in His infinite grace, has provided these prophecies, not to tantalize us with distant dreams, but to fill our hearts with hope, to stir within us a deep and abiding delight in the world He is preparing. He has unveiled far more about the new heavens and earth than most believers realize. A testament to God's love for us is His desire for us to know the glories that await us and to anticipate the day when we will dwell in His presence, in a world made new. We should not neglect these precious revelations. Instead, we should delve into the prophetic scriptures, seeking to understand the fullness of God's plan and embrace the hope that He has set before us. In understanding the Millennium, we understand Heaven itself, and we are filled with hope.

Chapter IV

The Millennial Temple

One of the most controversial passages of the Bible when it comes to interpretation is a prophecy that vividly portrays a grand Temple yet to be realized. I speak, of course, of Ezekiel 40-48. This prophesied Temple, described in meticulous detail, has never been built on earth. And yet, we know that God's prophetic word is infallible and incapable of falsehood. Therefore, we must conclude that it will be fulfilled in the future. Given its apparent connection to New Jerusalem, the city where God Himself will dwell (Ezekiel 48:35), it is most likely that this Temple will be established during the Millennial Reign of Christ.

Something that sets this prophecy apart is its specificity. There is no hint of symbolism and no suggestion of metaphor or analogy. Ezekiel's words are clear, direct, and detailed. For example, in Ezekiel 45:13-15 God lays out the offerings He expects in this new temple:

> This is the offering that you shall offer: a sixth of an ephah from a homer of wheat; a sixth of an ephah from a homer of barley; and the prescribed portion of oil (namely, the bath of oil), a tenth of a bath from each kor (which is ten baths or a homer, for ten baths are a homer); and one sheep

from each flock of two hundred from the watering places of Israel—for a grain offering, for a burnt offering and for peace offerings, to make atonement for them.

If this passage is to be interpreted symbolically, what grounds do we have for interpreting any other passage of scripture literally? What is the spiritual significance of "a homer of wheat"? What does "a sixth of an ephah" signify? What historical event is symbolized by "the bath of oil"? Why the "tenth" part of a bath? Who or what does "one sheep from each flock of two hundred" represent? What are the "watering places of Israel" a metaphor for? Most commentators who advocate for a symbolic interpretation of Ezekiel's Temple prudently avoid answering these questions. They recognize the absurdity of attempting to assign symbolic meanings to such precise details. And for those few who do venture to offer interpretations, the result is a cacophony of conflicting opinions, as varied as the commentators themselves. This is not how true Biblical prophecy operates.

If such prophecies, with their meticulous detail, are to be allegorized as mere symbols, subject to endless, conflicting interpretations, then what is the purpose of such a prophecy? What good is a message that no one can decipher, a riddle without a solution? Imagine that I were to deliver a prophecy concerning the United States Capitol. I declare that within ten years, a new Capitol building will rise, complete with eight elevators, each measuring precisely ten feet by eight feet by twelve feet, powered by Mitsubishi motors. Ten years pass, and no such structure appears. Instead, I offer a symbolic explanation. "The elevators," I pronounce, represent the growth of Apostolic Pentecostal churches. "Eight" signifies new beginnings. "Ten feet" represents the time period. "Eight feet" symbolizes the number of countries experiencing major earthquakes during that time period. "Twelve feet" is metaphorical for the "true Israel of God." And the "Mitsubishi motors" are allegorical for the power of our salvation. Would you consider me a true prophet who speaks with the authority of God? Absolutely not. Anyone could make "prophecies" like these.

True Biblical prophecy is, by its very essence, clear, understandable, and observable when it comes to pass. It is a hallmark of God's authority, a testament to His perfect knowledge of the future, and something that no mere mortal can replicate (Isaiah 41:23 and 46:10). *Anyone* can utter a "prophecy" where those who heard the prophecy believed it required a literal fulfillment, and then claim the prophecy was fulfilled allegorically or spiritually. But this is not the way of our God. Such ambiguous prophecies would do nothing to prove His authorship. Instead, He delivers prophecies that are fulfilled in the way they were naturally understood when given, thereby displaying His sovereign power and perfect foresight.

    This is the pattern we observe in the prophecies of God that have already found their fulfillment. In Genesis 18:10, God prophesied that Sarah would bear a son within a year. This prophecy was fulfilled literally as it was understood, not symbolically (Genesis 21:1-3). In Joshua 8:1, God prophesied that Israel would conquer Ai. This prophecy, too, was fulfilled according to its natural interpretation, not allegorically (Joshua 8:1-29). In 2 Chronicles 20:14-20, God, through Jahaziel, prophesied that a vast Edomite army would be destroyed without a fight. This also had a literal fulfillment, not a symbolic one (2 Chronicles 20:24). In Zechariah 9:9, God prophesied that Israel's King would ride into Jerusalem on a donkey. This was fulfilled in exactly the way that the prophecy foretold (Matthew 21:3-11). In Acts 23:11, Jesus prophesied to Paul that he would bear witness in Rome. Unsurprisingly, this prophecy was fulfilled literally as well (Acts 28:14-16).

Heaven and New Jerusalem

Examples like these are far too numerous to list. So why would Ezekiel's prophecy be an exception? Why would it not be fulfilled in the way it was naturally understood when it was given? When every other prophecy of God can be understood by its recipients and those who see its fulfillment, why would Ezekiel's prophecy remain shrouded in mystery, subject to a multitude of conflicting proposed allegorical fulfillments, having as many interpretations as there are commentators?

It is far more probable and far more consistent with the pattern established by other prophecies made and brought to pass by our God, that He will fulfill the prophecy of Ezekiel 40-48 in the manner it was naturally understood when it was given. And there is no hint in the text that Ezekiel or his audience would have understood this prophecy to be symbolic, metaphorical, or allegorical.

The primary reason many resist this literal interpretation lies not in the text itself, but in theological presuppositions and cherished doctrines that they hold above the plain reading of God's Word. If Ezekiel's Temple is indeed rebuilt in Israel, and the Israelites once again offer sacrifices and observe the ceremonial law, it would strongly suggest premillennialism (the belief that Jesus returns *before* or at the beginning of the Millennial Reign) and some form of dispensationalism (the belief that God interacts with Israel and the church in different ways, and that God has a plan for both) are true. However, it would be a death blow to belief systems such as postmillennialism (the belief that Jesus returns *after* the Millennial Reign), amillennialism (the belief that the Millennial Reign is essentially synonymous with the church age and that we are in the Millennium right now), preterism (the belief that most or all of God's prophecies were fulfilled with the destruction of Jerusalem in A.D. 70), and covenant theology (also known as replacement theology and supersessionism, which is the belief that God's covenant with the church has replaced or superseded His covenant with Israel).

It is integral for each of these doctrines to allegorize God's promises to Israel and to deny that God could ever sanction Israel's future participation in animal sacrifices. Those who cling to these theological constructs, prioritizing them above the clear pronouncements of Scripture, are compelled to interpret this prophecy about a future Temple as symbolic, even though no one would naturally come to this conclusion from a plain reading of the text. To acknowledge its literal fulfillment would force them to relinquish their unbiblical theological positions and to dismantle the very foundations of their false belief systems. They must, therefore, twist the words of Ezekiel, to find an allegorical meaning where none is intended.

Those who believe Ezekiel 40-48 is symbolic primarily offer Hebrews 10:10-18 in support of their position, which says,

Heaven and New Jerusalem

By this will we have been sanctified through the offering of the body of Jesus Christ once for all. Every priest stands daily ministering and offering time after time the same sacrifices, which can never take away sins; but He, having offered one sacrifice for sins for all time, sat down at the right hand of God, waiting from that time onward until his enemies be made a footstool for His feet. For by one offering He has perfected for all time those who are sanctified. And the Holy Spirit also testifies to us; for after saying, "This is the covenant that I will make with them after those days, says the Lord: I will put my laws upon their heart, and on their mind I will write them," He then says, "and their sins and their lawless deeds I will remember no more." Now where there is forgiveness of these things, there is no longer any offering for sin.

They argue that this passage teaches the cessation of animal sacrifices forevermore. Therefore, they conclude, Ezekiel's prophecy, though seemingly clear, cannot be interpreted naturally, like all other prophecies in the Bible, but must be relegated to the realm of figurative and symbolic interpretation. However, those who use this text in this manner show that they don't understand the purpose of the sacrifices in Ezekiel's Temple or any previous temple in Israel; they do not even understand what they are reading in Hebrews, conveniently ignoring a verse which disproves their entire position.

Ezekiel's prophecy indeed speaks of animal sacrifices and of atonement for sin (Ezekiel 40:39 and 45:15-20), mirroring the practices of Israel's past (e.g., Leviticus 16:34). But the linchpin, the crucial verse they sidestep, is Hebrews 10:11: "Every priest stands daily ministering and offering time after time the same sacrifices, which can *never* take away sins" (emphasis added). And further, Hebrews 10:12 proclaims that Jesus' sacrifice was "for all time." Herein lies the crux of the matter: no animal sacrifice, whether offered in ancient Israel or future Israel, can ever atone for sin.

All animal sacrifices are memorial, pointing either forward to Christ's once-for-all sacrifice (as in ancient Israel) or backward to that event (as in the Millennial Temple). Thus, the animal sacrifices in Ezekiel's Temple will not be atoning for sin any more than the sacrifices in Israel's previous Temples.

The point of Hebrews 10 is to refute those who believed that animal sacrifices actually possessed the power to atone for sin, a power they never held. Ironically, those who use Hebrews 10 to argue against the literal fulfillment of Ezekiel's Temple are making the very same error as the original audience of Hebrews. They believe that animal sacrifices *actually did* atone for sin in Israel's past and that a reinstitution of animal sacrifices in Ezekiel's

Heaven and New Jerusalem

Temple would be for the purpose of trying to make atonement for sins in place of Christ's sacrifice. In so doing, they miss the main point that the writer of Hebrews sought to convey. The sacrifices in Ezekiel's Temple, like those of old, will be a memorial, a reminder of the ultimate sacrifice of Christ, not a means of atoning for sin.

A parallel exists between the memorial sacrifices of Ezekiel's Temple and the sacred practice of communion in the church. They are, in essence, two expressions of remembrance of the ultimate sacrifice. Consider the words of Paul in 1 Corinthians 11:26: "For as often as you eat this bread and drink the cup, you proclaim the Lord's death until He comes." When we partake of communion, we are not, as some errant denominations believe, literally sacrificing Christ again. We are simply memorializing His death and His once-for-all sacrifice, the atoning act that secured our salvation.

Heaven and New Jerusalem

In the same way, the sacrifices that will be offered in Ezekiel's Temple are not intended to actually atone for sin. They are, rather, a memorial and a reminder of the Lamb who was slain, the Lamb who took away the sins of the world. Just as we, in the church, partake of the bread and the cup, remembering Christ's sacrifice, so too will the Israelites offer sacrifices in the Millenial Temple, remembering and celebrating the same redemptive act. Both communion and the Millennial sacrifices are acts of remembrance, acts of worship, and acts of proclamation. They point to the cross, to the empty tomb, and to the risen Savior. They declare, in their own unique ways, the truth of Christ's sacrifice, the power of His blood, and the hope of our salvation.

Fascinatingly, Hebrews 8:1-5, a passage of profound significance, reveals that Christ ministers in a literal Temple, a sanctuary that exists in Heaven *right now*, a Temple of which Israel's earthly Temples were but a shadow and copy.

> Now the main point in what has been said is this: we have such a high priest, who has taken His seat at the right hand of the throne of the Majesty in the heavens, a minister in the sanctuary and in the true tabernacle, which the Lord pitched, not man. For every high priest is appointed to offer both gifts and sacrifices; so it is necessary that this high priest also have something to offer. Now if He were on earth, He would not be a priest at all, since there are those

who offer the gifts according to the Law; who serve a copy and shadow of the heavenly things, just as Moses was warned by God when he was about to erect the tabernacle; for, "see," He says, "that you make all things according to the pattern which was shown you on the mountain."

Is it not then possible, even probable, that this heavenly Temple, this "true tabernacle," of which the earthly temples are mere shadows and copies, will descend to earth at the commencement of the Millennial Reign? Is it not likely that this is the very Temple Ezekiel beheld in his vision? The connection is compelling. The heavenly Temple is the dwelling place of our

Heaven and New Jerusalem

High Priest, the source of true worship, and may well become the centerpiece of the Millennial earth, alongside New Jerusalem.

In addition to New Jerusalem, this Temple will be a place where God will establish His throne and will dwell among His people forever (Ezekiel 43:7-9, Revelation 21:3, and Revelation 22:3). However, it is important to note that the prophecy does not state that animal sacrifices will continue eternally. We can reasonably presume that they will cease when sin and death are finally and completely abolished at the end of the Millennium (1 Corinthians 15:25-26). But from the dawn of the Millennium onward, this Temple will serve as an immeasurable blessing to humanity. It will be known as "a house of prayer for all the peoples," a sanctuary where all the earth's inhabitants, regardless of their nationality, can come to worship God and experience His presence (Isaiah 56:6-7). Indeed, many foreigners will be granted land in Israel, adjacent to the Temple, and will be treated as native-born Israelites, sharing in Israel's inheritance (Ezekiel 47:22-23).

There will be no vestige of the "court of the Gentiles" or the "court of women," the man-made barriers that unjustly separated those made in the image of God from His presence. These courts, never sanctioned by God's Law or anywhere else in Scripture, were sinful inventions, born of true racism and misogyny. In the Millennial Temple, all people, regardless of

Heaven and New Jerusalem

gender, race, nationality, or age, will be welcomed without partiality or segregation. There will be no veil and no barrier to God's presence, for His glory will be fully visible and accessible to all mankind. This Temple, then, will be a beacon of unity, a symbol of God's love, a place where all nations will gather to worship the one true God, and a place where the dividing walls of hostility will be forever dismantled.

Chapter V

The Lives of the Saints in Heaven and New Jerusalem

Now that we have laid the groundwork and explored the foundational truths concerning Heaven found in the Scriptures, let us turn our gaze to the unfolding panorama of life in the Kingdom and the glorious reality that awaits us. From the moment the wedding feast concludes, and Christ descends to earth, the saints, His faithful ones, will commence their reign alongside Him. As warriors in the heavenly armies, the vanguard of the divine invasion, their first task will be to subdue the wicked and to execute God's righteous judgment. Psalm 149, a prophetic glimpse into this momentous day, declares,

> Let the high praises of God be in their mouth, and a two-edged sword in their hand, to execute vengeance on the nations and punishment on the peoples, to bind their kings with chains and their nobles with fetters of iron, to execute on them the judgment written; this is an honor for all His godly ones. Praise the LORD! (Psalm 149:6-9)

Malachi 4:2-3 also contributes,

Heaven and New Jerusalem

"But for you who fear My name, the sun of righteousness will rise with healing in its wings; and you will go forth and skip about like calves from the stall. You will tread down the wicked, for they will be ashes under the soles of your feet on the day which I am preparing," says the LORD of hosts.

Imagine the awe-inspiring privilege of being a warrior in the Lord's army on that day at the battle of Armageddon, when He brings judgment and vengeance upon the wicked. Even those among us who have no experience with weaponry or warfare will

become formidable soldiers, for it is God Himself who will train our hands for war and our fingers for battle (Psalm 144:1). And let us not forget a crucial detail: these saintly warriors will be immortal, possessing an unmistakable tactical advantage over their mortal foes.

Heaven and New Jerusalem

This day of reckoning is foretold in Isaiah 24:21-22 which says,

> So it will happen in that day, that the LORD will punish the host of heaven on high, and the kings of the earth on earth. They will be gathered together like prisoners in the dungeon, and will be confined in prison; and after many days they will be punished.

This is the day of Armageddon, the day when the Lord will bring judgment upon the wicked rulers, the corrupt lawmakers, the powerful oppressors, and all men who have aligned themselves with the Antichrist. They will be the special targets of God's wrath and the recipients of His righteous indignation. Isaiah 10:1-4 amplifies this solemn warning:

> Woe to those who enact evil statutes and to those who constantly record unjust decisions, so as to deprive the needy of justice and rob the poor of My people of their rights, so that widows may be their spoil and that they may plunder the orphans. Now what will you do in the day of punishment, and in the devastation which will come from afar? To whom will you flee for help? And where will you leave your wealth? Nothing remains but to crouch among the captives or fall among the slain.

Heaven and New Jerusalem

When the Lord and His saints descend upon the earth, a great humbling of human pride will take place. Isaiah 2:11-12 speaks of this day:

> The proud look of man will be abased and the loftiness of man will be humbled, and the LORD alone will be exalted in that day. For the LORD of hosts will have a day of reckoning against everyone who is proud and lofty and against everyone who is lifted up, that he may be abased.

The arrogant, the wicked, and those who have exalted themselves above God and their fellow man will be utterly cut off. Their possessions and their ill-gotten gains will be redistributed, given to the poor, the meek, and the humble (Proverbs 2:22 and 15:25, Isaiah 13:9, Habbakuk 2:8, and Zephaniah 3:11). Included in this fate are those who are rich in this life, but who have used their wealth to oppress the poor and who have placed their trust in earthly riches rather than in God (Luke 12:13-21, 1 Timothy 6:17-19, and James 5:1-6). James 5:5, a prophetic indictment against these wicked rich people, declares, "You have lived luxuriously on the earth and led a life of wanton pleasure; you have fattened your hearts in a day of slaughter."

Imagine the dawn of a new era, the earth cleansed of wickedness, renewed by the very hand of God. And then, descending from the heavens, a sight to behold: New Jerusalem, the very throne of God, our eternal home. This will be the dwelling

Heaven and New Jerusalem

place of the saints, our "base of operations" for all eternity as we extend the dominion of Christ over the earth and all creation. This colossal city, a marvel of divine architecture, will be filled with beautiful dwellings, prepared for us by our Lord Himself (John 14:2). Righteous mortals from among the nations and their rulers will bring their glory into its gates (Revelation 21:24). The city's splendor will be beyond our wildest imaginations, so fabulously wealthy and magnificent that even its main street will be paved with pure gold (Revelation 21:21). But the true glory, the heart of this celestial city, will be the very presence of God Himself,

dwelling among us, His people (Revelation 21:3 and Ezekiel 48:35). Imagine the happiness of walking those golden streets, of dwelling in those beautiful homes, and of communing face to face with our God, our King, and our Savior.

In that day, Jesus will be the unchallenged king over all the earth (Zechariah 14:9). And we, the saints who have risen with Him, will serve as His ambassadors, His ministers, His servants, and His priests, extending His kingdom to the farthest reaches of

Heaven and New Jerusalem

the earth (Isaiah 61:6 and Revelation 1:6, 5:9-10). Daniel 7:18, a prophetic promise, assures us, "The saints of the Highest One will receive the kingdom and possess the kingdom forever, for all ages to come." Revelation 2:26-27 echoes this truth,

> He who overcomes, and he who keeps My deeds until the end, to him I will give authority over the nations; and he shall rule them with a rod of iron, as the vessels of the potter are broken to pieces, as I also have received authority from My Father.

Like Daniel 7:18, Revelation also emphasizes the eternality of our reign: "and they will reign forever and ever" (Revelation 22:5). Daniel 12:3, a vision of our glorified state, proclaims, "Those who have insight will shine brightly like the brightness of the expanse of heaven, and those who lead the many to righteousness, like the stars forever and ever." We will shine like the stars, reflecting the glory of God to illuminate the darkness and expand His influence to the ends of the universe. We will reign with Christ forever and ever. This is not a fleeting moment of glory, but an eternal inheritance, a reign that knows no end, and a dominion that will never fade.

The Bible gives some hints about the practicalities of this glorious reign. What will it look like to rule alongside our King? For many saints, this reign will involve the administration and governance of cities and nations.

Heaven and New Jerusalem

Recall the parable Jesus told in Luke 19:11-27, the story of the faithful servants and their entrusted talents. In that parable, the king rewarded those servants who had been faithful with small sums of money by granting them authority over multiple cities. Though a parable, its message rings clear: upon His return, God will bestow great responsibility and honor upon those saints who have proven faithful in the little things they have been entrusted with in this life. And why wouldn't this great responsibility and honor include the literal governance of cities as the parable suggests? Why couldn't it include the governance of entire nations or even distant planets? This, too, would be in keeping with the truth expressed in the parable.

This rulership could encompass a wide range of duties: making administrative decisions that impact the lives of citizens, overseeing agricultural and construction projects, guiding and directing public servants, providing spiritual leadership, and performing countless other esteemed tasks. Imagine the privilege of serving as a righteous ruler and a steward of God's kingdom in a world restored. Imagine the joy of using your God-given gifts and talents to bless and serve others, to build up the kingdom of God, to reflect the glory of your King. This is not a mere fantasy, but a divine promise and a glorious reality that awaits those who are faithful to the end. Our reign with Christ will be a reign of service, a reign of love, and a reign of eternal significance.

Another facet of our glorious reign with Christ is the sacred duty of serving as judges. Paul, in his rebuke to the Corinthian church for their practice of taking disputes between believers before secular courts, posed several penetrating questions:

> Or do you not know that the saints will judge the world? If the world is judged by you, are you not competent to constitute the smallest law courts? Do you not know that we will judge angels? How much more matters of this life? (1 Corinthians 6:2-3)

Heaven and New Jerusalem

In the Millennial Reign, we, the saints, will indeed serve as judges, hearing both civil and criminal cases and rendering righteous decisions. Because we will be perfected in righteousness, impartial in our judgments, and intimately knowledgeable of God's Law, we will be the most just and discerning judges the earth has ever known. Imagine the privilege of administering justice, of upholding truth, and of ensuring equity in a world restored to God's perfect order.

Paul's words reveal an even more astonishing reality: we will also be entrusted with the responsibility of judging angels. The nature of these cases is not explained by Paul, but we can be certain that many of these cases will be of far greater significance and intrigue than any case ever heard on earth to the present date. What profound matters will we adjudicate? What celestial disputes will we resolve? We can only speculate, but we can be assured that our judgments will reflect the wisdom and righteousness of our King. We will reign with Christ, not only as kings, but as judges, upholding His Law

Heaven and New Jerusalem

and ensuring that there is equity and justice in His dominion to the farthest reaches of His creation.

Another vital role that we will hold in the Millennial Reign is that of God's agents of justice, His ministers who bear the sword in accordance with Romans 13:1-7. We will execute His commands and enforce His Law, ensuring compliance with His directives. This role is not limited to the day of Armageddon, when we wield "two-edged swords" and execute "the judgment written" upon the nations (Psalm 149). Though the wicked will be purged at Armageddon, pockets of rebellion will flare up during the Millennium. Mortals and even nations will stray from the path of righteousness (Isaiah 65:20, Zechariah 14:18, and Revelation 20:8). In some instances, God Himself will intervene, executing judgment upon the wicked (Isaiah 19:22 and Zechariah 14:16-19). In others, He will delegate this duty to humans (Zechariah 13:2-3).

Heaven and New Jerusalem

When Revelation 2:26-27 prophesies that God "will give authority over the nations" to the overcoming saints, and that they "shall rule them with a rod of iron, as the vessels of the potter are broken to pieces," we must take God at His word. The saints will possess genuine authority, and they will enforce submission with rods of iron (weapons), if need be. These saints will be the epitome of law enforcement, the most righteous and effective officers the world has ever known.

Unlike the many unprincipled, egotistical officers of our present age, they will be incorruptible, perfectly just, completely humble, and utterly impartial. They will protect and commend the innocent, and they will never turn a blind eye to oppression. They will be instruments of God's wrath against the small remnant of evil that dares to raise its head during the Millennium. They will embody all that God intended for His ministers who bear the sword. Resurrected, immortal, possessing immense power and wisdom, they will be highly effective in their duties, making resistance futile. By comparison, the best of today's law enforcement agents will seem like children playing with plastic badges and toy guns. Such will be the power and authority of God's ministers in the Millennial Reign.

In our present time, law enforcement and priesthood fall on the opposite ends of the career spectrum. In New Jerusalem, we will be both. It is possible that some resurrected saints will serve as

Heaven and New Jerusalem

priests within the Temple described in Ezekiel 40-48. However, the majority of the saints will probably function as priests in the broader sense described in 1 Peter 2:5: "You also, as living stones, are being built up as a spiritual house for a holy priesthood, to offer up spiritual sacrifices acceptable to God through Jesus Christ." Even today, those who believe in Christ can be described as priests because of our spiritual access to God and our ability to intercede for others through prayer. Furthermore, empowered by the

Heaven and New Jerusalem

indwelling Holy Spirit, we are able to offer the sacrifices described in Hebrews 13:15-16:

> Through Him then, let us continually offer up a sacrifice of praise to God, that is, the fruit of lips that give thanks to His name. And do not neglect doing good and sharing, for with such sacrifices God is pleased.

Imagine how much more effectively we will be able to perform these priestly functions after our resurrection, when we are no longer hindered by our struggle against sin. Our praise will be more fervent, our prayers will be more powerful, and our service will be more beneficial to others.

In Heaven, reigning with Christ, exercising authority, and administering justice will not be the exclusive domain of men. There will be many resurrected female saints who will judge and rule the nations, just as Deborah, the prophetess of old who led an entire nation, judged court cases, and even commanded men in battle (Judges 4-5). Women are just as much "heirs of the grace of life" (1 Peter 3:7) as men. All the promises made to the saints concerning their role in the Kingdom of Heaven were given without any distinction between gender.

When Revelation 22:4 declares, "they will see his face," it does not add, "but only men will see his face; women will not." In the same way, when Revelation 22:5 proclaims, "they will reign forever and ever," it does not add, "but only men will reign;

women will not." The same holds true for the promise that the saints will exercise authority over the nations and rule them with rods of iron (Revelation 2:26-27). There is no statement, hint, or implication that only a certain demographic of saints will participate in these activities. These promises are made to all the saints, without partiality. Female saints will participate fully in the administration of the Kingdom of God, using their God-given gifts and talents to serve, to lead, to judge, and to rule, reflecting the glory of their King in all that they do.

What will happen to this divine government after the end of the Millennium, when sin and death have been completely abolished? Even then, there will be a need for righteous rule and for just administration. Though adversarial and criminal lawsuits will be no more, decisions affecting multiple parties will still require adjudication. Imagine a group of saints desiring to construct a dam. Such a project would impact those residing or working upstream and downstream. A wise and discerning saint acting as a righteous judge would be needed to weigh the considerations and to ensure fairness and equity for all involved.

Even in the perfected state, anarchy is not God's plan. There will always be a hierarchy of rulers and judges, a structure of authority, and a divinely ordained order. But these rulers will be unlike the typical rulers of this present era. They will not be

Heaven and New Jerusalem

tyrants, nor will they be harsh taskmasters. Jesus, in Luke 22:25-26, taught us,

> The kings of the Gentiles lord it over them; and those who have authority over them are called 'Benefactors.' But it is not this way with you, but the one who is the greatest among you must become like the youngest, and the leader like the servant.

In Heaven, this teaching will be fully embodied. The rulers will be the quintessence of servant leadership, compassionate and selfless leaders who are a delight to serve under. They will emulate the humility and service of their King, Jesus Christ, who came not to be served, but to serve.

Heaven and New Jerusalem

We will not be ruling from our own personal nebulous cloud: there are dwelling places and homes that await us in the new earth. It is likely that, wherever we reign, we will have homes in the cities and nations under our care, in addition to our residences in New Jerusalem.

This is a truth that should shape our lives today. We should live with a keen awareness of these future homes. Jesus, in Luke 16:9, counsels us, "And I say to you, make friends for yourselves by means of the wealth of unrighteousness, so that when it fails,

they will receive you into the eternal dwellings." What does this mean? It means that we should use the resources of this world, even the "wealth of unrighteousness," to do good and to bless

Heaven and New Jerusalem

others, not for the fleeting rewards of this present life, but for the eternal rewards that await us.

We should sow seeds of kindness, generosity, and compassion, so that when we enter our eternal inheritance, we will be welcomed into the Heavenly homes of those we have helped in this life. In this way, our good deeds will precede us and our love will pave the way for our eternal welcome. Imagine the joy of being greeted by those we have served and sharing fellowship in their Heavenly homes over a banquet. This is not a call to be self-seeking, but a call to eternal perspective. We should live with eternity in our hearts, knowing that our actions today have eternal rewards.

Beyond ruling and reigning, what will fill our days in Heaven? Certainly, there will be an abundance of peace and a profound rest for the weary souls of the saints (Matthew 11:28 and Isaiah 57:1-2). Yet, our eternity will not be one of idle repose. We will spend our days serving God, engaging in joyful, purposeful work (Revelation 22:3). Remember that God created each of us with unique personalities, interests, talents, and passions. These gifts, untainted by sin, are all good, bestowed upon us by our loving Creator (James 1:17) for His glory. If you excel in mathematics, in public speaking, or in writing, God will put these talents to use in Heaven. If you find joy in cooking, gardening, tennis, or ice skating, you will serve God by perfecting these skills

Heaven and New Jerusalem

in His presence. God crafted you to love these things, and you can honor Him simply by doing these things well.

If you cherish bike riding, hiking, reading, theological discussions, or building campfires with friends, there will be ample time for each of these activities in Heaven. Apart from sin, these activities are good, purposed by God for our enjoyment. And in Heaven, they will be even better, far exceeding the joys we experience on this present earth. If we can offer thanks to God for these things now (Colossians 3:17), how much more will our gratitude overflow in the Kingdom of Heaven? If we can perceive

Heaven and New Jerusalem

the goodness of God in how he has created our bodies, personalities, talents, and interests in this life, how much more glorious will these things be in the resurrection? Imagine the satisfaction of using our talents in perfect harmony with God's will and the joy of experiencing our favorite activities in their perfected, sinless state.

As our interests and passions are perfected, we too will have a glorious transformation: our mortal bodies will be replaced by immortal, resurrection bodies. Paul, in his discourse on the resurrection in 1 Corinthians 15:35-49, unveils the splendor of this future reality. He reveals that our resurrected bodies will be imbued with immense power, bearing the image of the last Adam, Jesus Christ. We will receive bodies like Christ's glorified resurrection body (Philippians 3:21). And let us be clear: Christ's resurrected body was undeniably real and physical. Ghosts and spirits cannot consume food as He did after His resurrection (Luke 24:42-43). Yet, His resurrected body also possessed supernatural abilities, such as teleportation (John 20:19). Therefore, it is entirely possible, even likely, that we, the resurrected saints, will possess superpowers as well. Imagine the possibilities!

Beyond their beauty, their might, their glory, and their immortality, our bodies will bear visible marks as a seal of God's marriage to us. We will have the name of God tattooed on our foreheads (Revelation 22:4), a testament of our belonging to Him.

Heaven and New Jerusalem

Elsewhere on our bodies, God will also tattoo the name of New Jerusalem and the new name of Jesus Christ (Revelation 3:12). Then we will know first-hand the kind of love described in Song of Solomon 8:6-7, which sings,

Put me like a seal over your heart, like a seal on your arm. For love is as strong as death, jealousy is as severe as Sheol; its flashes are flashes of fire, the very flame of the LORD. Many waters cannot quench love, nor will rivers overflow it; if a man were to give all the riches of his house for love, it would be utterly despised.

Perhaps the most wonderful truth of all is this: our new, resurrected bodies will never again experience pain, sorrow, or death (Revelation 21:4). No more tears, no more suffering, no more separation from our loved ones. We will be forever free from sin and forever dwelling in the presence of our God.

The question of marriage in the resurrection weighs heavily on the hearts of many Christians. Jesus speaks of this matter in Luke 20:34-36:

Heaven and New Jerusalem

The sons of this age marry and are given in marriage, but those who are considered worthy to attain to that age and the resurrection from the dead, neither marry nor are given in marriage; for they cannot even die anymore, because they are like angels, and are sons of God, being sons of the resurrection.

Some fear that the dissolution of earthly marital bonds will be a loss, a sorrow in the midst of eternal joy. Why will earthly marriages cease in Heaven? It is because we will be united in a far greater marriage, a marriage to Christ Himself. Paul, in 2 Corinthians 11:2, reveals this truth: "For I am jealous for you with a godly jealousy; for I betrothed you to one husband, so that to Christ I might present you as a pure virgin." And again, in Ephesians 5:25-32, Paul eloquently portrays the relationship between Christ and the church as a sacred marriage:

> Husbands, love your wives, just as Christ also loved the church and gave Himself up for her, so that He might sanctify her, having cleansed her by the washing of water with the word, that He might present to Himself the church in all her glory, having no spot or wrinkle or any such thing; but that she would be holy and blameless. So husbands ought also to love their own wives as their own bodies. He who loves his own wife loves himself; for no one ever hated his own flesh, but nourishes and cherishes it,

just as Christ also does the church, because we are members of His body. For this reason a man shall leave his father and mother and shall be joined to his wife, and the two shall become one flesh. This mystery is great; but I am speaking with reference to Christ and the church.

Finally, Revelation 19:7-9 prophesies of the glorious marriage of the saints to Christ:

"Let us rejoice and be glad and give the glory to Him, for the marriage of the Lamb has come and His bride has made herself ready." It was given to her to clothe herself in fine linen, bright and clean; for the fine linen is the righteous acts of the saints. Then he said to me, "Write, 'Blessed are those who are invited to the marriage supper of the Lamb.'"

Since we, the saints, are members of the Bride of Christ, we will be united to Him in marriage and will not be married to anyone else. Our earthly marriages, though beautiful and sacred, are but shadows of this greater union.

For those who have longed for the tender embrace of a spouse, yet have not found that joy in this earthly life, let this truth comfort and encourage you. The marriage of Christ and His Church, a union in which we all will partake, will be the most rapturous, intimate, and happy relationship imaginable. Those of you who have never known what it means to be "in love" will at last experience this feeling, and will experience it to a far greater

Heaven and New Jerusalem

degree than it has ever been experienced in any relationship in human history. All your years of loneliness and sorrow will not be worthy of comparison to even one day of your glorious marriage to Christ (Romans 8:18). As Paul observes in 1 Corinthians 7:29-31,

> Brethren, the time has been shortened, so that from now on those who have wives should be as though they had none; and those who weep, as though they did not weep; and those who rejoice, as though they did not rejoice; and those

Heaven and New Jerusalem

who buy, as though they did not possess; and those who use the world, as though they did not make full use of it; for the form of this world is passing away.

After the short years of our wandering in the shades of this earth have come to an end, all that will remain for us is true, everlasting life, intimacy, and riches in our marriage to Christ. This is a great comfort to those who have much sorrow and disappointment in this life, while it can sometimes be a stumbling block to those who have been given much.

For those who have tasted the sweetness of earthly marriage, who have found a beloved companion, the thought of separation can be a source of deep anguish. But let us consider a few truths that may ease your troubled hearts. First, remember that in Heaven, free from the corrupting influence of sin and human

Heaven and New Jerusalem

frailty, the bond between earthly spouses will be strengthened, purified, and deepened beyond anything we can comprehend. Consider the words of Ellicott's Commentary on Matthew 22:30:

> Will there, we ask, be no continuance there of the holiest of the ties of earth? Will the husband and the wife, who have loved each other until death parted them, be no more to each other than any others who are counted worthy to obtain that life? Will there be no individual recognition, no continuance of the love founded upon the memories of the past? The answer to all such questionings is found in dwelling on the "power of God." The old relations may subsist under new conditions. Things that are incompatible here may there be found to co-exist. The saintly wife of two saintly husbands may love both with an angelic, and therefore a pure and unimpaired affection.[8]

In other words, the love that binds you together in this life will not be extinguished, but transformed, perfected, and elevated to a level of love and delight that you cannot imagine. Although you will no longer be married to each other, your relationship will not be lost, but transfigured. The limitations and imperfections of earthly love will be replaced by a love that is pure, selfless, and eternal. The memories you share, the bonds you have forged, will not be erased, but woven into the tapestry of your eternal relationship with Christ and with one another. Your love story,

Heaven and New Jerusalem

begun on earth, will continue in Heaven, a story of redemption, restoration, and eternal happiness.

Second, regarding saints who have fallen asleep, Scripture emphasizes that we will be *together* with them *forever*. This precious reminder is given in a passage meant specifically to comfort those who grieve the loss of loved ones (1 Thessalonians 4:13-18), a comfort that most assuredly extends to grieving spouses. In Heaven, the sting of separation will be no more. There will be no more final goodbyes, because resurrected, immortal saints can no longer perish.

We will continue to enjoy delightful fellowship with our spouses, a fellowship that will never end. Some spouses may see each other every day in Heaven, their companionship a constant source of joy. It is equally possible that some will choose to remain together, their lives intertwined and their fellowship unbroken, for all eternity.

Heaven and New Jerusalem

But even if some former spouses meet only once a week for various reasons, consider this: once a week, forever, is an infinite amount of time. If a couple spends four hours together every Sabbath day for eternity, the amount of time they will share together literally cannot be comprehended by a human mind, because it is infinite. Regardless of the frequency of our reunions, we can cling to the unwavering promise of 1 Thessalonians 4:17, which assures us that we will be together, and this togetherness will endure forever.

Lastly, some people need to be exhorted to remember this fact: God, and God alone, can and will bring your spouse happiness in a way that neither you nor anything else in all creation can. God is the Creator of your spouse, her very Maker. He knows her intimately, more deeply than any human being ever could. He has numbered every hair on her head (Luke 12:7) and every cell in her body. He knows her innermost thoughts and her deepest desires. As the Author of her personality, the Architect of her soul, He knows precisely what will delight her and what will bring her the most profound and lasting happiness. He will shower her with unimaginable wonders, experiences tailored to her heart, moments of divine communion that only the two of them will share. He will give her a new name (Revelation 2:17), a name known only to her and to Him, a name that speaks of her true identity and her divine

Heaven and New Jerusalem

purpose. Regarding this new name, George MacDonald, with his insightful wisdom, proposed,

> God's name for a man must then be the expression in a mystical word—a word of that language which all who have overcome understand—of his own idea of the man, that being whom he had in his thought when he began to make the child, and whom he kept in his thought through the long process of creation that went to realize the idea. To

tell the name is to seal the success—to say, "In thee also I am well pleased."⁹

Let us remember that first and foremost, your spouse was created to enjoy God and to be enjoyed by God. Only secondarily was she created to enjoy others and to be enjoyed by others. Therefore, if possible, try to let go of your fears on this matter and, instead, trust in the boundless love and wisdom of God, who will care for your spouse with a tenderness and a depth of understanding that surpasses all human capacity.

All of these truths apply to you as well. In the last chapter of C.S. Lewis' *The Problem of Pain*, he writes the following gem of literature:

> I am considering not how, but why, He makes each soul unique. If He had no use for all these differences, I do not see why He should have created more souls than one. Be sure that the ins and outs of your individuality are no mystery to Him; and one day they will no longer be a mystery to you. The mould in which a key is made would be a strange thing, if you had never seen a key: and the key itself a strange thing if you had never seen a lock. Your soul has a curious shape because it is a hollow made to fit a particular swelling in the infinite contours of the Divine substance, or a key to unlock one of the doors in the house with many mansions. For it is not humanity in the abstract

that is to be saved, but you—you, the individual reader, John Stubbs or Janet Smith. Blessed and fortunate creature, your eyes shall behold Him and not another's. All that you are, sins apart, is destined, if you will let God have His good way, to utter satisfaction… Your place in heaven will seem to be made for you and you alone, because you were made for it—made for it stitch by stitch as a glove is made for a hand.[10]

Eighty years earlier, George MacDonald wrote,

I would rather be what God chose to make me, than the most glorious creature that I could think of. For to have been thought about—born in God's thoughts—and then made by God, is the dearest, grandest, most precious thing in all thinking.[11]

This truth resonates deeply with the intimate portrayal of our relationship with God in Psalm 139:13-18:

For You formed my inward parts; you wove me in my mother's womb. I will give thanks to You, for I am fearfully and wonderfully made; wonderful are Your works, and my soul knows it very well. My frame was not hidden from You, when I was made in secret, and skillfully wrought in the depths of the earth; Your eyes have seen my unformed substance; and in Your book were all written the days that were ordained for me, when as yet there was not

Heaven and New Jerusalem

one of them. How precious also are Your thoughts to me, O God! How vast is the sum of them! If I should count them, they would outnumber the sand. When I awake, I am still with You.

We struggle now, in this earthly life, to grasp the immensity of God's affection and the depth of His care for us and all the saints. But a day is coming when the fog will clear and the shadows will flee, and we will see Him face to face. As Paul declares in 1 Corinthians 13:12: "For now we see in a mirror dimly, but then face to face; now I know in part, but then I will know fully just as I also have been fully known."

Imagine the sheer delight of that moment, the overwhelming joy of fully comprehending the boundless love of our God. How wondrous it will be to gaze upon our Divine Lover, to behold His face in all its glory (Revelation 22:4)! And think of the joy

of seeing our loved ones, their faces radiant with indescribable happiness, sharing in this divine communion. How incredible it is that this perfect love, this eternal fellowship, will never end, but will endure forever (1 Corinthians 13:13)! We will dwell in the light of His love, bathed in His glory, forever and ever. Let us, then, anticipate this glorious day, this unveiling of divine love, with hearts overflowing with gratitude. Let us live in the light of this hope, knowing that our present sufferings are but fleeting shadows compared to the eternal glory that awaits us.

Lastly, although nothing can surpass the happiness of beholding our God face to face, one more aspect of Kingdom life that we can greatly anticipate is the thrill of space travel, exploration, and colonization, an endless frontier of discovery. Isaiah 9:7, speaking of Jesus, prophesies, "There will be no end to the *increase* of His government…" (emphasis added). This is not a mere figure of speech, but a promise of eternal growth. In the fullness of time, Christ's government will encompass the entire earth, His dominion extending to every corner of our planet. But for His government to continue its *increase*, to fulfill the prophecy of Isaiah, His kingdom must expand beyond the boundaries of our planet.

God will not allow the kingdoms of this age, who have already been to space, to accomplish more technologically than His Kingdom will. Modern governments will continue sending humans

Heaven and New Jerusalem

deeper and deeper into space until Jesus returns (and, at His return, He will send out angels to gather His elect "from the farthest end of the earth to the farthest end of heaven," according to Mark 13:27, meaning that there will be saints residing at the farthest ends of heaven, perhaps in planes, spaceships, the International Space Station, or on Mars, who will not miss the rapture despite their distance from earth). But Christ's government, with all of its technological advancements, will send immortal humans with superpowers deeper into space than today's scientists can even see with their most powerful telescopes.

And consider this: the universe itself is constantly expanding, and our God, the Creator of all things, possesses the power to continually create new worlds, new galaxies, new realms of existence. Imagine the endless possibilities: new challenges to overcome, new species of animals and plants to discover, possibly even new races of unfallen beings, made in God's image, to encounter.

This expansion and adventure will truly continue for eternity, an endless journey of discovery and dominion. And without a doubt, we, the saints, will be a part of this thrilling mission. We will explore the vastness of space, we will colonize new worlds, and we will extend the dominion of Christ to the farthest reaches of His creation. We will be His ambassadors, venturing into the unknown, expanding His kingdom, and glorifying His name throughout the cosmos. This is not a mere flight of fancy, but a certain glimpse into the eternal future, a future filled with adventure, discovery, and the boundless happiness of serving our God in the vast expanse of His creation.

Chapter VI:

The Geography and Society of Heaven and New Jerusalem

Having now journeyed through the wonders of our eternal lives in the new heavens and the new earth, we will now turn our focus to the details of its geography and society which are revealed in the Word of God. It is crucial to understand that the thousand-year reign of Christ and His saints will unfold as a progressive, step-by-step process. While the Lord's second coming will bring about an instantaneous transformation, a sudden and dramatic shift in the spiritual and physical realms, the full restoration will be a gradual unfolding.

In one moment, Satan, the "god of this age" will be bound, his power to deceive the nations curtailed (until the end of the Millennial, when he will be released for a brief season). Earth will be ushered into a new era, under a new government, with a new King. The very elements of creation will be transformed, a radical remaking of all things. Yet, as Revelation 21:5 declares, God will be "*making* all things new" (emphasis added), a process that will unfold over time. As 1 Corinthians 15:25 states, "For He must reign *until* He has put all His enemies under His feet" (emphasis added). The ultimate goal of this gradual restoration is to undo the devastating effects of the Fall and to restore earth and humanity to their Edenic purpose. For mankind, this means a return to our original calling: to cultivate and care for the garden (Genesis 2:15) and to exercise dominion over all creation (Genesis 1:26-29).

How will God accomplish this gradual restoration? He will work primarily through the life-giving water of the river of life and the fruit of the tree of life. This river, flowing from the throne of God in New Jerusalem (Revelation 22:1), will run northward, reaching His throne in the Temple. From here, the waters will divide, one half rushing eastward into the Dead Sea, and the other westward into the Mediterranean Sea (Ezekiel 47:1-3, 8, Joel 3:18, and Zechariah 14:8). These waters will transform the seas, turning them into fresh, life-giving waters, teeming with an abundance of sea creatures (Ezekiel 47:8-9).

It is evident that these waters possess both physical and spiritual healing properties (Revelation 22:17). However, it appears that their potency is most concentrated in or around New Jerusalem, since those who thirst are invited to "come" and drink. This suggests a specific location that people must travel to if they wish to partake in the healing benefits of the water of life. It is possible that, after the end of the Millennium and into eternity future, all the waters of the earth will be transformed into the water of life. But if this were the case before the Millennium's end, the

Heaven and New Jerusalem

invitation to "come" and drink would seem superfluous, as the waters would be readily available everywhere.

On both banks of the river of life, there will be trees of life (Ezekiel 47:12 and Revelation 22:2). These trees bear fruit every month for eternity, signifying that there will always be enough of its fruit for everyone. The fruit will never be scarce and never unavailable due to changing seasons. These trees, it seems, are the very same as the tree of life that graced the Garden of Eden (Genesis 2:9, 3:22, 3:24), which provided eternal life through its sustenance. Like the water of life, the fruit of these trees possesses both physical and spiritual healing properties, bringing restoration to the nations (Revelation 22:2). During the Millennial Reign, should anyone desire to eat of the tree of life and live forever, they will be free to do so, provided they come to Jesus and wash their robes (Revelation 22:14). And let us not forget the open invitation, the gracious call to all who thirst: "The Spirit and the bride say, 'Come.' And let the one who hears say, 'Come.' And let the one who is thirsty come; let the one who wishes take the water of life without cost" (Revelation 22:17).

Lamentably, many mortals in the Millennium will reject this gracious invitation, the free gift of eternal life, because they refuse to come to Christ and be cleansed by His blood. They will cling to their sins, preferring the fleeting pleasures of their perversions to the pure, eternal happiness offered by Christ. They would rather perish in their rebellion than live forever in the light of God's love. These souls, tragically, will face the consequences of their choice. They will be cut off in their youth (Isaiah 65:20), or they will live until the end of the Millennial age, only to be deceived by Satan, to join in a futile rebellion against God in New Jerusalem, and to be consumed by fire from the heavens (Revelation 20:9).

But there will be many righteous mortals who will gladly accept the free gift of eternal life. They will come to Christ, they will wash their robes in His blood, and they will partake of the fruit of the tree of life and the water of life. They will never taste death and never experience the sting of separation from God. They will live, flourish, and be happy in the presence of their Savior. And in the fullness of time, at the culmination of the Millennial age, they will be clothed with glorified, immortal bodies (1 Corinthians 15:24), transformed into the likeness of their Lord.

The transformative power of the tree of life and the water of life will be profound. The cumulative effects will reshape the nations, bringing healing and restoration to every facet of human existence. As time unfolds, the impact will touch every aspect of life: religion, health, economics, politics, art, culture, geography, climate, and agriculture.

Human health will flourish (Isaiah 66:14), and people's lives will be "like a watered garden" (Jeremiah 31:12). The crippled and diseased will be healed, and the outcasts will be praised, honored, and brought into the community (Zephaniah 3:19). Humans will live as long as trees (Isaiah 65:22), especially the righteous, who will never die. Entire cities, young and old alike, will participate in communal dancing, their voices raised in happy songs of praise for God's wondrous deeds (Jeremiah 31:4, 13 and Isaiah 35:10). Psalm 45, a prophetic glimpse of Jesus' reign (according to Hebrews 1:8), speaks of magnificent ivory palaces and stringed instruments, filling the air with celestial music. People

Heaven and New Jerusalem

will delight in the fruits of their labor, no longer fearing theft or calamity (Isaiah 65:21-23). The nations will bring their "glory and honor" into New Jerusalem (Revelation 21:26), meaning that all that is glorious and honorable in their cultures—music, dance, dress, food, architecture, language, and literature—will be present, but magnified, perfected, and infinitely more glorious. Human languages will be purified, free from the filth and darkness that plagues our present world (Zephaniah 3:9). Rulers, even mortal ones, will no longer oppress their people (Ezekiel 45:8-9). The earth will be saturated with the knowledge of the Lord (Isaiah 11:9 and Habbakuk. 2:14). All nations will become God's people (Isaiah 19:24-25) and, marvelously, all nations will witness the glory of God (Isaiah 66:18-19). This is the vision of the Millennial age, a

time of unprecedented blessing, a time of restoration, and a time when the glory of God will fill the earth as the waters cover the sea.

The Millenium is not only for adults; there are precious children who will inherit this world of unparalleled blessing. This Millennial age will be a time of extraordinary happiness for them. From the very inception of this era, no infants or children will ever again taste the bitterness of death (Isaiah 65:20, 23), and there will be no more abortions or miscarriages. During this time, all children will be taught of the Lord and nurtured by Him from the moment of their conception, experiencing both physical and spiritual well-being (Isaiah 54:13). They will play without fear and without the possibility of serious injury, even venturing near the dens of poisonous snakes and reaching in without harm (Isaiah 11:8-9). And consider the sweet prophecy of Zechariah 8:3-5, a glimpse into the heart of that blessed age:

> Thus says the LORD, "I will return to Zion and will dwell in the midst of Jerusalem. Then Jerusalem will be called the City of Truth, and the mountain of the LORD of hosts will be called the Holy Mountain." Thus says the LORD of hosts, "Old men and old women will again sit in the streets of Jerusalem, each man with his staff in his hand because of age. And the streets of the city will be filled with boys and girls playing in its streets."

Heaven and New Jerusalem

New Jerusalem will not be a sterile, adults-only space, a place of somber formality. It will be alive with the happy sounds of children, their laughter echoing through the streets and their uninhibited play being seen everywhere. The Holy City will be known as a haven for children and a place where they are welcomed, cherished, and embraced. "For the kingdom of heaven belongs to such as these," Jesus declared (Matthew 19:14). No one will bar children from the city and no one will keep them from

Heaven and New Jerusalem

Jesus. They will be with Him, basking in His presence and growing in His love, their lives a testament to the happiness and innocence of a restored world.

The rhythm of life in the Millennial age and beyond will be characterized by a society which is *primarily* agrarian and a return to humanity's original calling: to cultivate and tend the garden. Micah 4:3-4 declares,

> And He will judge between many peoples and render decisions for mighty, distant nations. Then they will hammer their swords into plowshares and their spears into pruning hooks; nation will not lift up sword against nation, and never again will they train for war. Each of them will sit under his vine and under his fig tree, with no one to make them afraid, for the mouth of the LORD of hosts has spoken.

Amos 9:13-14, a promise of abundance and restoration, proclaims,

> "Behold, days are coming," declares the LORD, "When the plowman will overtake the reaper and the treader of grapes him who sows seed; when the mountains will drip sweet wine and all the hills will be dissolved. Also I will restore the captivity of My people Israel, and they will rebuild the ruined cities and live in them; they will also plant vineyards and drink their wine, and make gardens and eat their fruit."

Heaven and New Jerusalem

Other passages which amplify this theme of agricultural abundance and peaceful cultivation during the Millennium include Joel 3:18, Jeremiah 31:5, and Zechariah 13:4-5. Imagine an earth where there the sounds of war, violence, and destruction have been completely replaced by the gentle lowing of sheep and cattle, loud cicadas on summer nights, the whistle of the wind in the trees, whippoorwills singing at dusk, and the happy laughs of friends and family around a fire after a fulfilling day of working off the land. How wonderful this future will be!

Isaiah 32:20, in a prophetic glimpse of what appears to be the Millennium, declares, "How blessed will you be, you who sow beside all waters, who let out freely the ox and the donkey." In that blessed era, the practices of our present age, the massive monoculture fields and the crowded animal farms where creatures are confined in tight enclosures, will no longer be allowed. Instead, individuals and communities will sustain themselves, growing the food they need through small fields, horticulture, permaculture, and free-ranging herds.

As the earth is transformed, remade by God's hand, the land will become increasingly fruitful and productive. It will be possible for humanity to simply tend the garden, without the sweat and toil that has been our lot since the Fall (Genesis 3:17). No longer will we be burdened by the curse of Adam, the struggle to wrest sustenance from a resistant earth. Instead, we will work in partnership with God's creation, nurturing its growth and enjoying its abundant yield.

Not only will mortals tend the garden, but we can expect that this will be a major focus of Jesus, His government, and the immortal saints. Ecclesiastes 5:9 reminds us, "A king who cultivates the field is an advantage to the land." As the best king in history, Christ will also be the best agriculturist. He will be all that the first Adam was supposed to be and more. He will be the ultimate gardener, the perfect steward, and the one who brings forth abundance and beauty from the earth, restoring it to its original glory. Imagine the joy of working in harmony with God's creation, of partaking of its bounty, and of seeing the land flourish under the care of righteous hands. This is the promise of the Millennial age.

While agriculture will play a primary role in the Millennium, it will not be the sole work performed by humanity. Amos 9:14, as we have seen, speaks of the rebuilding of ruined

Heaven and New Jerusalem

cities. This implies a need for skilled craftsmen, surveyors, masons, carpenters, architects, engineers, and painters, all working together to restore and beautify the dwelling places of humanity. Isaiah 60:9 prophesies of ships traversing the seas, carrying people to distant shores. This necessitates that there will be sailors who navigate the waters and shipbuilders who construct their vessels. And if there are sailing ships, why not spaceships, astronauts, and rocket scientists? In a realm where we will live eternally, where scientific discovery and technological innovation will flourish, where we are called to subdue all creation, we can expect a multitude of new and unimaginable occupations.

Heaven and New Jerusalem

The curse of toil and the burden of weariness will be lifted. Work will no longer be a source of frustration or unhappiness. There will be no more tyrannical bosses and no more disagreeable coworkers. Instead, we will find purpose, joy, and camaraderie in our labor. Our leaders will be true servant-leaders, caring for us with genuine love and compassion. Our fellow saints, our coworkers, will be filled with the fruit of the Spirit, being perfectly kind, patient, and loving, free from jealousy, arrogance, rudeness, and selfishness (1 Corinthians 13:4-5). Our work will be a source of delight, a reflection of God's creative nature, a testament to His goodness and grace. We will labor with happiness, serve with love, and glorify God in all that we do.

One last beautiful aspect of the Millennium and eternal state that we will look at are the special blessings for the nation and people of Israel, who are God's chosen people according to Romans 11:28. Due to God's enduring love for this people, the covenants He made with their forefathers, and the especially grievous historical injustices and atrocities they have been subjected to by wicked men from seemingly every nation on earth, He will pour out unique and abundant blessings upon them for all eternity. The Word of God reveals that all nations of the earth will serve Israel, showering them with riches and honor. And, should any nation refuse to do so, it will face divine judgment. Isaiah

60:10-12, a powerful declaration of God's faithfulness to Israel, proclaims,

> Foreigners will build up your walls, and their kings will minister to you; for in My wrath I struck you, and in My favor I have had compassion on you. Your gates will be open continually; they will not be closed day or night, so that men may bring to you the wealth of the nations, with their kings led in procession. For the nation and the kingdom which will not serve you will perish, and the nations will be utterly ruined.

This passage presents a challenge to those who harbor hatred for the Jews, those who would truly rather perish in Hell than obey God by serving the people of Israel. It also confronts the errors of replacement theology, which claims these prophecies are merely metaphorical, referring to the church. God has never, and will never, subject the church to His wrath (1 Thessalonians 5:9). While He may allow tribulation to refine the church, He does not pour out His wrath upon us as He has upon Israel. This passage must be read with an open mind, without preconceived agendas. It means precisely what it says: although God struck Israel in wrath for refusing to accept their Messiah, He will bring about their total salvation (Romans 11:26) and will pour out His unmerited favor on them, commanding all nations to serve Israel during the Millennial age and to shower blessings on His chosen people, and those who

Heaven and New Jerusalem

refuse will face divine punishment. This is not a matter of human preference or political opinion, but a declaration of God's will and a testament to His enduring faithfulness to His chosen people.

Isaiah 45:14 foretells,

Thus says the LORD, "The products of Egypt and the merchandise of Cush and the Sabeans, men of stature, will come over to you and will be yours; they will walk behind you, they will come over in chains and will bow down to you; they will make supplication to you: 'Surely, God is with you, and there is none else, no other God.'"

The very nations that once oppressed and persecuted Israel, will come to acknowledge the God of Israel as the one true God. Mortals from every corner of the earth, those who survive the Day of the Lord through God's protective grace, will finally recognize the divine power of the God of Israel. They will witness the miraculous deliverance of the remnant of Israel, rescued from the clutches of the Antichrist and the armies of the world. They will see the righteous vengeance that God exacted upon Israel's enemies, and they will tremble before His awesome power. This is why Isaiah 49:26 declares,

> I will feed your oppressors with their own flesh, and they will become drunk with their own blood as with sweet wine; and all flesh will know that I, the LORD, am your Savior and your Redeemer, the Mighty One of Jacob.

Joel 3:1-2, a solemn declaration of God's judgment, asserts,

> In those days and at that time, when I restore the fortunes of Judah and Jerusalem, I will gather all the nations and bring them down to the valley of Jehoshaphat. Then I will enter into judgment with them there on behalf of My people and My inheritance, Israel, whom they have scattered among the nations; and they have divided up my land.

Isaiah 60:14 adds,

Heaven and New Jerusalem

The sons of those who afflicted you will come bowing to you, and all those who despised you will bow themselves at the soles of your feet; and they will call you the city of the LORD, the Zion of the Holy One of Israel.

Furthermore, Zephaniah 3:19-20 declares,

"Behold, I am going to deal at that time with all your oppressors, I will save the lame and gather the outcast, and I will turn their shame into praise and renown in all the earth. At that time I will bring you in, even at the time when I gather you together; indeed, I will give you renown and praise among all the peoples of the earth, when I restore your fortunes before your eyes," says the LORD.

Finally, Zechariah 2:8-10 promises,

For thus says the LORD of hosts, "After glory He has sent me against the nations which plunder you, for he who touches you, touches the apple of His eye. For behold, I will wave My hand over them so that they will be plunder for their slaves. Then you will know that the LORD of hosts has sent Me. Sing for joy and be glad, O daughter of Zion; for behold I am coming and I will dwell in your midst," declares the LORD.

Heaven and New Jerusalem

The oppressors of the Jews will be consumed by their own wickedness, their own violence turned against them. All flesh will know that the Lord, the God of Israel, is the Savior and Redeemer, the Mighty One of Jacob. This is not a matter of human pride or nationalistic arrogance, but a matter of God's sovereign choice of the people of Israel and a testament to His faithfulness to His covenant people. The nations will come to recognize this truth and, when they do, they will bow before the God of Israel, because all those who came against God and His chosen people Israel will have been slaughtered by the Lord and the Heavenly armies, their bodies becoming food for the birds (Ezekiel 38:14-16, 39:17-21 and Revelation 19:21).

During the Millennium and afterwards, people from all nations will pilgrimage to New Jerusalem. The deep longing to be in God's presence will draw people from every corner of the earth, and they will bring their treasures and their wealth to Israel (Isaiah 60:11). And consider this: the nations will make this pilgrimage *every week* on the Sabbath day (Isaiah 66:23)! Interestingly, this implies a remarkable advancement in transportation technology, a means to facilitate the movement of billions of mortal humans very quickly. This will be the time prophesied by Zechariah 8:23, which proclaims, "Thus says the LORD of hosts, 'In those days ten men from all the nations will grasp the garment of a Jew, saying, "Let us go with you, for we have heard that God is with you."'" Isaiah

60:3 adds, "Nations will come to your light, and kings to the brightness of your rising," a truth echoed in the majestic vision of Revelation 21:24-26. Micah 4:2 predicts,

> Many nations will come and say, "Come and let us go up to the mountain of the LORD and to the house of the God of Jacob, that He may teach us about His ways and that we may walk in His paths." For from Zion will go forth the law, even the word of the LORD from Jerusalem.

Further, Zephaniah 3:10, a promise of global worship, prophesies, "From beyond the rivers of Ethiopia My worshipers, My dispersed ones, will bring My offerings."

Moreover, all the nations of the world will gather in New Jerusalem to celebrate the Feast of Booths, a celebration of God's enduring faithfulness. Zechariah 14:16 affirms this truth:

> Then it will come about that any who are left of all the nations that went against Jerusalem will go up from year to year to worship the King, the LORD of hosts, and to celebrate the Feast of Booths.

Imagine the wonderful scene: people from every tribe, nation, and tongue, from every corner of the earth, dwelling together in tents, camping in perfect peace in the land of Israel. They will gather to worship the King, the Lord of hosts, their hearts overflowing with gratitude and praise. They will recount the stories of God's faithfulness, provision, and protection during their wanderings on earth. They will share testimonies of His grace, His mercy, His love, their voices blending in a symphony of adoration.

This will be a joyous occasion and a time of unparalleled fellowship, a celebration that will surpass all earthly festivals. It will likely be the holiday that people anticipate with the greatest longing, the event that fills their hearts with the most profound happiness. Think of the unity, the camaraderie, and the shared experience of camping in tents, a reminder of God's provision in the wilderness. Think of the songs of praise and the adoration that

Heaven and New Jerusalem

will ascend to Heaven, a sweet aroma to the Lord. This is the picture of a world redeemed, a world united in worship, and a world where the nations gather to celebrate the goodness and faithfulness of our God. Let us anticipate this glorious festival, this annual celebration of God's love, which will surely come to pass in the Millennium, with hearts filled with wonder and praise.

Let us now turn our hearts to the grand finale of Isaiah's prophecy. Isaiah 66:22-24, a powerful and poignant conclusion, declares,

Heaven and New Jerusalem

"For just as the new heavens and the new earth which I make will endure before Me," declares the LORD, "So your [Israel's] offspring and your [Israel's] name will endure. And it shall be from new moon to new moon and from sabbath to sabbath, all mankind will come to bow down before Me," says the LORD. "Then they will go forth and look on the corpses of the men who have transgressed against Me. For their worm will not die and their fire will not be quenched; and they will be an abhorrence to all mankind."

This passage, a fitting conclusion to the book of Isaiah, which contains so many prophecies about Heaven, New Jerusalem, and the Millennium, is an excellent capstone to our own reflections as well. How my heart yearns for that day, when all humanity, dwelling in perfect harmony, will journey to New Jerusalem, Sabbath after Sabbath, to bow before Yeshua Hamashiach—Jesus the Messiah—the Savior of Israel and all the world.

This will be the dawn of an eternal adventure, a story that unfolds with ever-increasing wonder, each year surpassing the last in its splendor and glory. This will be the true "golden age," the utopia that humanity has longed for, a reality far surpassing our wildest dreams. It will be anything but mundane and boring. It will be a vibrant, dynamic, ever-evolving experience, a journey into the depths of God's love, an exploration of His boundless creation and a participation in His eternal purpose for us. The new heavens and the new earth will endure forever, showing God's faithfulness, and will be a dwelling place of righteousness and a realm of unending happiness.

As we gather, Sabbath after Sabbath, to worship our King, we will remember the fate of those who rejected His love and the free offer of His grace, those who chose darkness over light, those who transgressed His Law, and those who oppressed the poor and God's chosen people, Israel. Their shame will be remembered and abhorred by the righteous forever. But for the saints who have received Christ's boundless grace, those who have embraced His free offer of salvation, there is an unshakable assurance. We can be confident, utterly confident, that the eternal riches He bestows upon us will never be lost, never be diminished, and never be taken away.

These promises are as certain and secure as the very establishment of the new heavens and the new earth. They are as steadfast as the covenant protection and kindness God has shown to the nation and people of Israel, a covenant that endures forever, never to be replaced, superseded, or annulled, no matter what Israel does, because God's favor to Israel and to us is without merit.

Just as the new heavens and the new earth will stand as a perpetual testament to God's creative power, just as His covenant

Heaven and New Jerusalem

with Israel will remain an eternal symbol of His faithfulness, so too will our inheritance and our eternal riches endure as a monument to His grace. There is no wavering, no uncertainty, and no possibility of loss. God cannot forget or forsake Israel (Isaiah 49:14-16), so neither can He forget or forsake us. Our salvation is not built on shifting sands, but on the solid rock of God's unchanging character and promises. Let us, then, rest in the assurance of His promises, let us rejoice in the security of His grace, and let us anticipate the eternal riches that await us in Heaven and New Jerusalem. For our God is faithful, His promises are sure, and our inheritance is secure, forever and ever.

BIBLIOGRAPHY

1. Lewis, C. (1952). *The Complete C.S. Lewis Signature Classics* (*Mere Christianity*). Pg. 46. HarperCollins.
2. Lewis, C. (1956). *The Chronicles of Narnia: The Last Battle*. Pg. 172. HarperCollins.
3. Lewis, C. (1956). *The Chronicles of Narnia: The Last Battle*. Pg. 170. HarperCollins.
4. Gulbekian, E. (1987). The Origin and Value of the Stadion Unit used by Eratosthenes in the Third Century B.C. *Archive for History of Exact Sciences*, *67*(5), 359-363. https://doi.org/10.1007/BF00417008
5. Ibid.
6. Sulley, H. (1887). *The Temple of Ezekiel's Prophecy*. Pg. 14. Self-published. https://antipas.org/library/Henry%20Sulley/Temple%20of%20Ezekiels%20Prophecy%20-%201887%20ed.pdf
7. Ibid, pg. 88.
8. Matthew 22 Ellicot's Commentary for English Readers. (n.d.). Bible Hub. https://biblehub.com/commentaries/ellicott/matthew/22.htm

9. Unspoken Sermons by George MacDonald: The New Name. (n.d.). The Literature Network.

   https://www.online-literature.com/george-macdonald/unspoken-sermons/5/

10. Lewis, C. (1940). *The Complete C.S. Lewis Signature Classics* (*The Problem of Pain*). Pg. 640. HarperCollins.

11. David Elginbrod by George MacDonald: Chapter XIX. The Ghost's Walk. (n.d.). The Literature Network.

    https://www.online-literature.com/george-macdonald/david-elginbrod/34/

www.ingramcontent.com/pod-product-compliance
Lightning Source LLC
Chambersburg PA
CBHW041621220426
43662CB00001B/9